PAUL'S VISION
FOR THE DEACONS:
ASSISTING THE ELDERS
WITH THE CARE
OF GOD'S CHURCH

Other books by Alexander Strauch include:

Biblical Eldership:
An Urgent Call to Restore Biblical Church Leadership

The Study Guide to Biblical Eldership:
Twelve Lessons for Mentoring Men for Eldership

Meetings That Work

The New Testament Deacon: Minister of Mercy

The Hospitality Commands

Agape Leadership:
Lessons in Spiritual Leadership from the Life of
R. C. Chapman (Coauthored with Robert L. Peterson)

Men and Women: Equal Yet Different

A Christian Leader's Guide to Leading With Love

Love or Die:
Christ's Wake-Up Call to the Church, Revelation 2:4

If You Bite and Devour One Another:
Biblical Principles for Handling Conflict

PAUL'S VISION FOR THE
DEACONS

ASSISTING THE
ELDERS WITH
THE CARE OF
GOD'S CHURCH

ALEXANDER STRAUCH

Lewis & Roth Publishers

Paul's Vision for the Deacons: Assisting the Elders with the Care of God's Church
ISBN-10: 0936083360
ISBN-13: 9780936083360
Copyright © 2017 by Alexander Strauch. All rights reserved.

Cover design: Bryana Mansfield

Printed in the United States of America
Fourth Printing 2020

Library of Congress Control Number: 2017940128

To receive a free catalog of books published by Lewis and Roth Publishers,
please call toll free 800-477-3239 or visit our website, *www.lewisandroth.org.*
If you are calling from outside the United States, please call 719-494-1800.

Lewis and Roth Publishers
P.O. Box 469
Littleton, Colorado 80160

Contents

ABBREVIATIONS

1. Old Testament

Gen.	Genesis	Ezra	Ezra	Dan.	Daniel
Ex.	Exodus	Neh.	Nehemiah	Hos.	Hosea
Lev.	Leviticus	Est.	Esther	Joel	Joel
Num.	Numbers	Job	Job	Amos	Amos
Deut.	Deuteronomy	Ps.	Psalm(s)	Obad.	Obadiah
Josh.	Joshua	Prov.	Proverbs	Jonah	Jonah
Judg.	Judges	Eccl.	Ecclesiastes	Mic.	Micah
Ruth	Ruth	Song	Song of	Nah.	Nahum
1 Sam.	1 Samuel		Solomon	Hab.	Habakkuk
2 Sam.	2 Samuel	Isa.	Isaiah	Zeph.	Zephaniah
1 Kings	1 Kings	Jer.	Jeremiah	Hag.	Haggai
2 Kings	2 Kings	Lam.	Lamentations	Zech.	Zechariah
1 Chron.	1 Chronicles	Ezek.	Ezekiel	Mal.	Malachi
2 Chron.	2 Chronicles				

2. New Testament

Matt.	Matthew	Phil.	Philippians	James	James
Mark	Mark	Col.	Colossians	1 Peter	1 Peter
Luke	Luke	1 Thess.	1 Thessalonians	2 Peter	2 Peter
John	John	2 Thess.	2 Thessalonians	1 John	1 John
Acts	Acts of the	1 Tim.	1 Timothy	2 John	2 John
	Apostles	2 Tim.	2 Timothy	3 John	3 John
Rom.	Romans	Titus	Titus	Jude	Jude
1 Cor.	1 Corinthians	Philem.	Philemon	Rev.	Revelation
2 Cor.	2 Corinthians	Heb.	Hebrews		
Gal.	Galatians				
Eph.	Ephesians				

3. Bible Translations

Bruce	F. F. Bruce, *Letters of Paul: An Expanded Paraphrase* (Grand Rapids: Eerdmans, 1965)
CSB	Christian Standard Bible
ESV	English Standard Version (Text Edition 2016)
GNC	Heinz W. Cassirer, *God's New Covenant: A New Testament Translation* (Grand Rapids: Eerdmans, 1989)
GNT	Good News Translation
Godby	W. B. Godby, *Translation of the New Testament*
Goodspeed	Edgar J. Goodspeed, *The Complete Bible: An American Translation*
KJV	King James Version
Moffatt	Moffatt New Testament
MSNT	R. F. Waymouth, *Modern Speech New Testament*
NASB	New American Standard Bible
NCV	New Century Version
NEB	The New English Bible
NIV	New International Version
NKJV	New King James Version
NLT	New Living Translation
NRSV	New Revised Standard Version
Phillips	J. B. Phillips, *The New Testament in Modern English*
REB	The Revised English Bible
RV	Revised Version of the Bible
TEV	Today's English Version
TNIV	Today's New International Version

4. Other Books

ACT	Ancient Christian Texts
BCBC	Believers Church Bible Commentary
BDAG	Walter Bauer, *A Greek-English Lexicon of the New Testament and Other Early Christian Literature*, 3rd ed., trans. W. F. Arndt and F. W. Gingrich, revised and edited by Frederick William Danker (Chicago: University of Chicago, 2000)
BNTC	Black's New Testament Commentary
CCE	Christ-Centered Exposition
CNTC	Calvin's New Testament Commentaries
EGGNT	Exegetical Guide to the Greek New Testament

HNTC	Holman New Testament Commentary
ICC	The International Critical Commentary
IVP	InterVarsity Press
IVPNTCS	IVP New Testament Commentary Series
LCL	Loeb Classical Library
MNTC	Moffatt New Testament Commentary
NAC	New American Commentary
NICNT	New International Commentary on the New Testament
NIDNTTE	*New International Dictionary of New Testament Theology and Exegesis*, 2nd ed.
NIGTC	New International Greek Testament Commentary
NTC	New Testament Commentary
TDNT	G. Kittel and G. Friedrich (eds.), *Theological Dictionary of the New Testament*
TLNT	C. Spicq, J. D. Ernest (trans. & ed.), *Theological Lexicon of the New Testament*
WBC	Word Biblical Commentary

What Do Deacons Do?

There seems to be no end to the opinions people have about the role of deacons in the church. Over the years, I have asked many people the question, "What do deacons do?" and have received a wide range of responses. It is quite confusing!

For example, when approaching a church I was visiting, I was greeted by a friendly man who was trimming bushes and mowing the grass. After a warm Christian greeting, he volunteered to tell me he was a deacon. I could see that he was a good man and proud to serve his church. So I asked, "What do deacons do?"

"Deacons," he replied, "care for the church's facilities. They make sure the building and grounds are presentable to the public."

While having lunch with a long-time friend who had recently become a deacon, I asked, "What do deacons do?"

"They're the governing board of the church," he answered. "Nothing happens in the church without the deacons' consent."

On another occasion, I was introduced to a man who identified himself as a church deacon. I asked, "What do deacons do?"

"Deacons lead the church's ministry teams," he said. "I'm the coordinator of the church's audio-visual team. Others coordinate the small-group ministry, the evangelism committee, or the building maintenance team."

Then I asked a biblical scholar, "What do deacons do?"

"Deacons can teach, preach, counsel, evangelize, manage church programs, and help the needy. They are models of servant leadership."

In addition to these answers, responses to my question about the responsibilities and activities of deacons have included everything from arranging flowers, leading political action groups, feeding the homeless, administering the Lord's Supper, handing out church bulletins, and helping the poor, to sharing in the pastoral responsibilities of the church. And in a few churches, anyone serving the church in any capacity is considered to be a deacon because the word *deacon* (Greek, *diakonos*) means *servant.* I suppose this viewpoint justifies the most amusing answer to my question about what deacons do: "I'm the coffee-bar deacon." In such cases, the title "deacon" is almost meaningless.

Among evangelical, Bible-believing Christians there exist widely divergent views on the role of deacons. Some churches do not even have deacons because they see no need for them. Of those that do have deacons, I have found that churches of the same denomination in the same city may have diametrically opposite views. In one church, for example, deacons are *the* governing board of the church. While across town in another church, deacons are the building maintenance crew.

My intention in writing this book is to encourage my dear deacon friends and fellow church leaders to think more critically about what they are saying and doing in light of what Scripture actually teaches (or does not teach) about deacons. Sadly, most of the literature I have read on this subject claims biblical authority but provides little or no biblical evidence or exegesis for the assertions made.

Whatever your view may be, I urge you to use this study to examine in detail the biblical facts on deacons and allow those facts to guide your thinking. This approach offers the opportunity to build broader agreement among Bible-believing churches as to what deacons do.

My intention in writing this book is to encourage my dear deacon friends and fellow church leaders to think more critically about what they are saying and doing in light of what Scripture actually teaches (or does not teach) about deacons.

THE BEREAN CHALLENGE

When Paul, the great missionary of the gospel message to the Gentile world, arrived in a new city, his customary practice was to first attend the local Jewish synagogue and present to his Jewish compatriots the good news of Jesus as Messiah as demonstrated through the Old Testament Scriptures. On Paul's second missionary journey, he visited the city of Berea in Macedonia (modern-day northern Greece) where he encountered a unique group. When the Berean Jews first heard Paul preach that Jesus was the long-awaited Messiah, they *eagerly received* the good news. But they *confirmed* his message as well:

> They received the word with all eagerness, examining the Scriptures daily to see if these things were so. Many of them therefore believed. (Acts 17:11–12)

The Berean Jews believed the Old Testament Scriptures to be the Word of God and thus divinely authoritative. For that reason, they critically examined the message of the great apostle Paul to see if it agreed with God's message as revealed in Holy Scripture. They were careful so as not to be misled, even by someone as great as Paul.

The Bereans were serious-minded Bible students. They knew that the Scriptures were written in such a way that they must be searched and studied diligently, so they examined the Scriptures daily. Furthermore, they were not blind traditionalists who were closed to fresh biblical insights. They were willing to change their minds when persuaded by thoughtful examination of the Scriptures.

I am citing the attitudes and diligence of the Bereans because the nature of this biblical study of deacons requires that we do as they did. We must exert effort in order to understand and absorb the scriptural arguments presented. If we approach our study of deacons with the attitudes and diligence of the Bereans, this study will be enlightening even if we cannot agree on all the details.

I am citing the attitudes and diligence of the Bereans because the nature of this biblical study of deacons requires that we do as they did. We must exert effort in order to understand and absorb the scriptural arguments presented.

There is another reason we need to conduct ourselves like the Bereans. It is not enough to study Scripture and discover truth. We must, by God's grace, confront our own traditions and opinions and when necessary make appropriate changes. From personal experience I know that changing long-standing, cherished church tradition is difficult, and this study will challenge some deep-seated opinions. That is why we need to adopt the Bereans' attitude. We need to be prepared to reevaluate our most treasured traditions in the light of God's Word and make appropriate changes wisely and courageously.

Deacons, prospective deacons, and the elders responsible for overseeing deacons will find the study guide to be a valuable complement to the book:

Paul's Vision for the Deacons: Study Guide
ISBN 978-093608335-3

I recommend that the church elders go through this guide before the deacons in order to supervise the deacons most effectively. The study guide is available from your local bookstore, many online retailers, or from Lewis & Roth Publishers.

Part One

WHAT ARE THE BIBLICAL
STARTING POINTS FOR DEACONS?

Paul and Timothy, servants of Christ Jesus,
To all the saints in Christ Jesus who are at Philippi, with the overseers and deacons.

Philippians 1:1

Deacons [*diakonoi*] likewise must be dignified, not double-tongued, not addicted to much wine, not greedy for dishonest gain. They must hold the mystery of the faith with a clear conscience. And let them also be tested first; then let them serve [verb form, *diakoneō*] as deacons if they prove themselves blameless. Their wives likewise must be dignified, not slanderers, but sober-minded, faithful in all things. Let deacons [*diakonoi*] each be the husband of one wife, managing their children and their own households well. For those who serve [verb form, *diakoneō*] well as deacons gain a good standing for themselves and also great confidence in the faith that is in Christ Jesus.

1 Timothy 3:8–13

Chapter 1

Paul's Instructions Regarding Deacons

A woman who was concerned about a friend of hers who had not attended church in a long time asked her pastor if he would call the man. She said, "If you ask him to be a deacon, maybe he would start coming to church again and get involved." Although the concerned lady meant well, her request shows a lack of understanding about the biblical requirements for deacons and the biblical significance of their office and role in the church.

Unfortunately, her lack of knowledge about deacons is not uncommon. Her request demonstrates the low view that many people have about deacons. But as we will soon see, there must be something very significant about the deacons' ministry that requires both specific, elder-like qualifications and verification of such qualifications by the church and its leaders. Not just anyone can be a deacon, and the diaconate (or deaconship) is not intended to be a means for involving people in the life of the church.

If we want to know what the responsibilities of deacons are and who qualifies to be a deacon, we must look at what Scripture says. But before we begin, we must consider who the apostle Paul is and why he wrote the letter of 1 Timothy. This background is necessary because Paul is the only New Testament writer who mentions deacons, and his instructions for deacons are found only in his first letter to Timothy.

PAUL, AN APOSTLE OF CHRIST JESUS

Paul was directly chosen by Jesus Christ to be an *apostle* (Greek, *apostolos*), which means he was a special authorized messenger, an emissary, or an envoy sent by Christ. He was not just a missionary, a church-growth advisor, or a brilliant scholar— although he was all of those. The apostle Paul was Christ's special ambassador to define, defend, and proclaim the gospel to the Gentile nations.[1] As such, he played a unique role in the foundation of the Christian faith.

In fact, one of the most momentous events at the dawn of Christianity was when Christ appeared to the young, zealous rabbi Saul on the Damascus road, which led to Saul's radical conversion to faith in Christ as Messiah. Shortly after that encounter, Jesus referred to Saul (who later took the name Paul) as "a chosen instrument of mine to carry my name before the Gentiles and kings and the children of Israel" (Acts 9:15). As Christ's ambassador (2 Cor. 5:20), the apostle Paul lived out the cruciform lifestyle of Christ for others to imitate.

Paul's gospel is Christ's gospel. What Paul teaches is what Christ teaches. What Paul commands is what Christ commands.

Thus, Paul did not fabricate the gospel message. He received it by direct revelation from the risen Lord Jesus Christ. Paul's gospel, then, is Christ's gospel. What Paul teaches is what Christ teaches. What Paul commands is what Christ commands. Paul's authority to give written instructions to the churches is Christ-given authority.

As "a Heaven-commissioned ambassador,"[2] Paul delivered authoritative teaching for conduct and life in the local church.[3] In conjunction with his close associate Luke, Paul wrote slightly over fifty percent of the New Testament. He is the master architect of much of the vocabulary and theological concepts regarding the gospel and the Church, which is evident in his two magisterial letters, Romans and Ephesians. He also has provided specific instructions regarding both elders and deacons. So let's begin our study by considering the urgent crisis in the church at Ephesus (in modern-day Turkey) that compelled Paul to write the letter of 1 Timothy.

PAUL AND THE LETTER OF 1 TIMOTHY: A RESPONSE TO A CRISIS IN THE CHURCH AND ITS LEADERSHIP

Our study on deacons will focus primarily on Paul's first letter to Timothy, which begins with Paul's declaration that he is "an apostle of Christ Jesus." He also notes that he is an apostle "by command of God":

> Paul, an apostle of Christ Jesus by command of God our Savior and of Christ Jesus our hope, to Timothy, my true child in the faith. (1 Tim. 1:1–2)

One biblical commentator succinctly captures the commanding force of Paul's opening declaration in 1 Timothy:

> It was right, therefore, [that Timothy] should feel that necessity was laid upon him; that the voice which speaks to him is that not merely of a revered instructor or a spiritual father, but of a Heaven-commissioned ambassador, who has a right to declare the divine will and rule with authority in the Christian church.[4]

This strong declaration was needed because five to seven years had passed since Paul's farewell meeting with the Ephesian elders

(Acts 20:17–38). Tragically, from around AD 57 to AD 64, the Ephesian elders had failed to protect the church from false teachers. This was a particularly dreadful failure because the local church is to be "a pillar and buttress of the truth" (1 Tim. 3:15), that truth being the glorious, good news message of salvation through Jesus Christ (1 Tim. 1:11). Instead, heretical teachings had become quite advanced in the church and had adversely affected every aspect of the life of the church.

The new teachings had caused fighting and arguing among the people, lack of prayer, improper behavior on the part of many toward one another, neglect of its destitute widows, and problems within the church's leadership. Paul even had to excommunicate two of the ringleaders of the heresy, Hymenaeus and Alexander (1 Tim. 1:20). Given this background, it is no wonder a strong sense of urgency and emotion permeates Paul's letter to Timothy. His beloved church was in the death grip of false teachers!

As one notable Bible expositor puts it:

> The church that Paul addresses had been torn apart by the false teachers, and much of this letter is aimed at putting the pieces back together.[5]

One of the likely causes for the upset in Ephesus was that unqualified, unfit people had become elders and deacons during Paul's absence.[6] Prominent in Paul's strategy for "putting the pieces back together," then, was *insisting that the church's elders and deacons be properly qualified and examined as to those qualifications before they served.* So in 1 Timothy 3:1–13, Paul sets down scriptural requirements for the church's overseers (= elders) and deacons, insisting that both groups be examined by the congregation and its leaders for fitness for office.

Specific Information Provided in Scripture

To prepare for our study, we need to review the biblical information on deacons and clarify the problems we all face in identifying the New Testament deacon.

1. Deacons Are First Mentioned in Paul's Greeting to the Church in Philippi.

Deacons appeared early in the history of the Christian movement, no later than the mid 50s. The frame of reference for this early date is that Christ's death, resurrection, and ascension occurred either in AD 30 or 33. The earliest mention of deacons—in plural form alongside the church overseers—is found in Paul's letter to the church in Philippi (in modern-day Greece):

> Paul and Timothy, servants of Christ Jesus, to all the saints in Christ Jesus who are at Philippi, with the overseers and deacons. (Phil. 1:1)

As was typical when Paul wrote to a local church, he addresses the entire church, not just the leaders. Here he uses one of his favorite designations for all Christians: "saints." By this all-important term he means, "God's holy people" (NIV), a people set apart for God's purposes and separate from the world's philosophy and immoral lifestyle.

But only in this letter does he add, "with the overseers and deacons." These officials are *together with the saints*. They are an integral part of the believing community. After this special mention of overseers and deacons, we hear nothing more about them in the letter, at least by these titles. It is the entire church's responsibilty, together with its overseers and deacons, to carry out Paul's instructions and to solve the growing problem of conflict within the church. As the terms themselves indicate, the overseers and deacons would have primary responsibility to provide the leadership needed for the congregation to carry out Paul's instructions.

2. Deacons Are Regulated by Paul's Instructions in 1 Timothy 3:8–13.

Both the churches in Ephesus and Philippi were founded, taught, and organized by Paul. Most New Testament information about deacons comes from one source: Paul's instructions to Timothy and the church in Ephesus, written sometime between the years AD 63 to 65. Therefore our study will center on 1 Timothy 3:8–13.

Prominent in Paul's strategy for "putting the pieces back together," then, was insisting that the church's elders and deacons be properly qualified and examined as to those qualifications before they served.

---

3. Deacons Are Always Mentioned After the Overseers.

In both Philippians 1:1 and 1 Timothy 3:1–13, deacons are paired with the overseers. When referenced together, deacons always follow the overseers in order of mention, suggesting that deacons work under the supervision of the church overseers.

More important, the terms *overseers* (Greek, *episkopoi*) and *deacons* (Greek, *diakonoi*) indicate that the deacons are subject to the overseers. The Greek term *overseer* denotes a superintendent, manager, or guardian. The Greek term *deacon* can mean servant, commissioned messenger, or agent of a superior.

Thus, the overseers do not need the deacons in order to function as overseers of the local church. The *episkopoi* can stand alone, however, the deacons must stand in relationship to some person or some body of people for direction: "From the nature of the terms, *episkopoi* could operate without *diakonoi*, but *diakonoi* could not operate without some such mandating functionary as an *episkopos*."[7] The overseers are not subordinate to servants or assistants, but the deacons are subordinate to the overseers.

"From the nature of the terms, *episkopoi* could operate without *diakonoi*, but *diakonoi* could not operate without some such mandating functionary as an *episkopos*." — John Collins

---

4. Deacons Are Required to Meet Specific Qualifications.

In 1 Timothy 3:8–12 Paul dictates the specific qualifications of a deacon. Many of the requirements listed for the deacons are the same or similar to those listed for the elders:

- Known to hold the mystery of the faith with a clear conscience
- Tested first and proven blameless
- Dignified
- Not double-tongued
- Not greedy for dishonest gain
- Not addicted to much wine
- Husband of one wife
- Wife who is faithful in all things
- Children and household managed well

It is important for us to realize that Paul shows as much concern for the deacons' eligibility as he does for the overseers' qualifications. As to the nature of deacons' duties, however, Paul provides no specific list of responsibilities.

5. Deacons Are Not Required to Teach.

Unlike overseers who must be "able to teach" (1 Tim. 3:2), and "able to give instruction in sound doctrine and also to rebuke those who contradict it" (Titus 1:9), Paul does not require that deacons be "able to teach." The fact that such abilities are not required of the deacons is very important to our investigation.

6. Deacons Are Required to Be Examined and Approved by the Church and Its Leaders.

Deacon candidates must be examined as to whether or not they possess the prescribed qualifications:

> And let them also be tested first; then let them serve as deacons
> if they prove themselves blameless. (1 Tim. 3:10)

The process of selecting, examining, and approving potential deacons requires time and effort, just as it does with potential elders. Paul insists that the church and its leaders carefully evaluate those it appoints as deacons.

We cannot account for deacon qualifications and the necessity for public examination unless deacons hold some official position of public trust or exercise some specialized ministry for which only certain people qualify. Thus there must be something very significant about the deacons' ministry that requires both specific, elder-like qualifications and verification of such qualifications by the church and its leaders.

7. Deacons Are Church Officeholders Like the Overseers.

We know that deacons are official church officeholders because of the following facts: Mention of deacons appears in the context of instructions on local church officials, not where spiritual gifts are addressed.[8] Deacons appear in context with the church overseers who are definitely church officeholders. Specific qualifications are stated as prerequisites for selection to be a deacon (1 Tim. 3:8–12). Deacons must be examined and found by others to be above reproach according to the biblical qualifications (1 Tim. 3:10). The term *diakonoi* is used in 1 Timothy 3 and Philippians 1 as a formal title, just as the title *overseer* is used of certain recognized church officials. Deacons have been recognized as a permanent office in the local church from the first century to the present time.

8. "Deacons" Is Plural.

Paul uses the plural form "deacons," not the singular form "deacon," in Philippians 1:1 and 1 Timothy 3:8, 12. This suggests that more than one deacon was needed in these churches and certainly allows for more than one deacon per church. It may also indicate that at times deacons work as a corporate body like the elders.

9. Deacons' Wives (or Women Deacons) Are Required to Meet Specific Qualifications.

As part of his instructions, Paul requires that deacons' wives meet certain character qualifications:

> Their wives likewise must be dignified, not slanderers, but sober-minded, faithful in all things. (1 Tim. 3:11)

Many scholars, however, believe that Paul is not referring to the deacons' wives, but to women deacons (equal to male deacons), or deaconesses (a separate group from male deacons), or women helpers (to the deacons and women of the church). But one's particular view of the women of 1 Timothy 3:11 does not ultimately affect the outcome of our study on what deacons do. We will probe the question of women deacons or deaconesses in Chapter 7 and the Appendix.

10. Deacons Can Gain Much Respect in the Eyes of the Church and Have Their Faith in Christ Deepened.

Paul says that deacons who serve well will gain an honorable and influential standing in the eyes of the people. They will also see their faith in Christ greatly enlarged, deepened, and emboldened:

> For those who serve well as deacons gain a good standing for themselves and also great confidence in the faith that is in Christ Jesus. (1 Tim. 3:13)

By promising such rewards, Paul gives his special endorsement to the role of deacons within the church.

We cannot account for deacon qualifications and the necessity for public examination unless deacons hold some official position of public trust or exercise some specialized ministry for which only certain people qualify.

---

11. Deacons Are Called *Diakonoi* in Greek.

The English word *deacon* is a transliteration of the Greek word *diakonos*. Of the twenty-one occurrences of *diakonos* in Paul's letters, the *English Standard Version* translates only three of them as *deacons* (Phil. 1:1; 1 Tim. 3:8, 12). In all other places in the Greek New Testament where *diakonos* appears, the ESV translates *diakonos* as either *servant* (eleven times)[9] or *minister* (seven times).[10]

One of the most critical questions in our study of deacons is: How is Paul using the Greek term *diakonos* in the two key passages? Is *diakonos* a table-servant metaphor for church officials, a commissioned messenger, or an assistant? This question is addressed in Chapter 3.

The *Diakon-* Word Group

Diakonos is pronounced dee-AH-ko-nos.

The plural form of *diakonos* is *diakonoi*, pronounced dee-AH-ko-noi.

The verb form of *diakonos* is *diakoneō*, pronounced dee-ah-ko-NEH-o.

The abstract noun form is *diakonia*, pronounced dee-ah-ko-NEE-ah.

In this study, it is important to know how to pronounce these three Greek words and to be able to distinguish the verb form, *diakoneō*, from the two noun forms, *diakonia* and *diakonos*.

Greek is an inflected language that changes the form of a word depending on how it is used by an author. For simplicity and consistency, the dictionary form of each word is cited, unless otherwise noted.

PAUL DOES NOT TELL US EVERYTHING

Now that we have surveyed the New Testament information about deacons, we still need to know: Who were the deacons? Why and how did they originate? What did they do? The problem is, Paul does not explicitly state who the deacons are or what they do. He states only what their qualifications are, the necessity for examination of their eligibility for office, and their promised rewards.

Admittedly, this lack of specific information is frustrating and has led to the widely diverse views held by Bible teachers and churches today. In fact, some scholars suggest that "there is insufficient evidence for determining" the role of deacons.[11] However, the fact that Paul does not further explain the deacons' role does not make identifying their role a hopeless pursuit. It simply means we must begin with a clear understanding of the role of the church overseers with whom the deacons are closely associated. Then we will be prepared to consider the term *diakonos* and its key context, 1 Timothy 3:1–13.

Key Points to Remember:

1. The three Greek words that are foundational to this study are: *diakonos* (noun), *diakoneō* (verb), and *diakonia* (abstract noun).

2. Deacons are qualified church officeholders, as are the overseers.

3. Deacons must be examined and approved by the church and its leaders.

4. The challenge for all of us is that Paul does not explicitly state who the deacons are, or what they do.

---

[1]Acts 9:15–17; 20:24; 22:14–15; 26:15–18; Rom. 1:5; 11:13; 15:15–18; 16:25–26; 1 Cor. 9:1–2; 11:23; 15:3–11; 2 Cor. 12:12; Gal. 1:1, 11, 16; 2:7–8; Eph. 3:1–13; 6:19–20; Phil. 1:16; Col. 1:25–27; 2 Thess. 2:15; 3:6, 14; 1 Tim. 1:11; 2:7; 2 Tim.

1:11, 13; 4:17; Titus 1:3.

[2]Patrick Fairbairn, *Pastoral Epistles* (1874; repr. Minneapolis: James & Klock, 1976), 70.

[3]1 Cor. 4:14–17; 7:17; 11:16, 23, 34; 14:36–38; 15:3; 16:1.

[4]Fairbairn, *Pastoral Epistles*, 70.

[5]Philip H. Towner, *1–2 Timothy & Titus*, IVPNTCS (Downers Grove, IL: InterVarsity, 1994), 123.

[6]1 Tim. 1:19–20; 5:19–25.

[7]John N. Collins, *Deacons and the Church* (Harrisburg, PA: Morehouse, 2002), 92.

[8]Rom. 12:4–8; 1 Cor. 12:1–31; 14:1–40; Eph. 4:7–16; 1 Peter 4:10–11.

[9]Rom. 13:4 (twice); 15:8; 16:1; 1 Cor. 3:5; 2 Cor. 6:4; 11:15 (twice), 23; Gal. 2:17; 1 Tim. 4:6.

[10]2 Cor. 3:6; Eph. 3:7; 6:21; Col. 1:7, 23, 25; 4:7.

[11]C. F. D. Moule, "Deacons in the New Testament," *Theology* 58 (1955), 405–07.

Part Two

OVERSEERS AND DEACONS

[You elders] pay careful attention to yourselves and to all the flock, in which the Holy Spirit has made you overseers, to care for the church of God, which he obtained with his own blood.

Acts 20:28

The saying is trustworthy: If anyone aspires to the office of overseer, he desires a noble task. Therefore an overseer must be above reproach, the husband of one wife, sober-minded, self-controlled, respectable, hospitable, able to teach, not a drunkard, not violent but gentle, not quarrelsome, not a lover of money. He must manage his own household well, with all dignity keeping his children submissive, for if someone does not know how to manage his own household, how will he care for God's church? He must not be a recent convert, or he may become puffed up with conceit and fall into the condemnation of the devil. Moreover, he must be well thought of by outsiders, so that he may not fall into disgrace, into a snare of the devil.

1 Timothy 3:1–7

This is why I left you in Crete, so that you might put what remained into order, and appoint elders in every town as I directed you—if anyone is above reproach, the husband of one wife, and his children are believers and not open to the charge of debauchery or insubordination. For an overseer, as God's steward, must be above reproach. He must not be arrogant or quick-tempered or a drunkard or violent or greedy for gain, but hospitable, a lover of good, self-controlled, upright, holy, and disciplined. He must hold firm to the trustworthy word as taught, so that he may be able to give instruction in sound doctrine and also to rebuke those who contradict it.

Titus 1:5–9

Chapter 2

THE CHURCH OVERSEERS, THE ELDERS

It might seem strange to include a chapter on church overseers in a book about deacons, but in order to understand deacons we must first accurately identify the New Testament overseers with whom the deacons are always linked. In fact, the position and role of the overseers (also called *elders* in the New Testament) provides an important key to understanding who the deacons are and what they do.

Identifying the role of the New Testament overseers (= elders) is especially important because in many churches today deacons are *the* governing board of the church. In such circumstances, deacons act as quasi-overseers. When deacons are made overseers and overseers are made deacons, the church is left with neither biblical overseers nor biblical deacons.

The Berean Christians would not put up with such confusion.[1] Just as they would have done, we also must search the Scriptures and press on until we settle on God-given, biblical answers as to who the overseers and deacons are and what God instructs them to do. My intent in this book is to correct some of the confusion and false statements made about deacons by faithfully addressing the texts of Scripture. Therefore, we will establish the foundation for our study with a brief survey of the New Testament's distinctive teaching on church overseers/elders.*

When deacons are made overseers and overseers are made deacons, the church is left with neither biblical overseers nor biblical deacons.

BIBLICAL OVERSEERS ARE ELDERS

The Greek word for *overseer* is *episkopos* (pronounced, ee-PIS-ka-pos), which was a well-known, commonly used designation for various kinds of officials. The word conveyed the idea of a superintendent or an official guardian. Paul uses *episkopos* (overseer) several times to describe local church officials:

Paul and Timothy, servants of Christ Jesus, to all the saints in Christ Jesus who are at Philippi, with the overseers [plural] and deacons. (Phil. 1:1)

[You elders] pay careful attention to yourselves and to all the flock, in which the Holy Spirit has made you overseers [plural], to care for [literally, shepherd] the church of God, which he obtained with his own blood. (Acts 20:28)

Appoint elders [plural] in every town as I directed you—if anyone [singular] is above reproach, the husband of one wife, and his children are believers and not open to the charge of debauchery or insubordination. For an overseer [singular], as God's steward,

---

*For more detailed information go to www.biblicaleldership.com or see Alexander Strauch, *Biblical Eldership: An Urgent Call to Restore Biblical Church Leadership* (Littleton, CO: Lewis and Roth, 1995).

must be above reproach. (Titus 1:6–7)

Paul also uses the related noun, *episkopē,* to define the work or position of an overseer:

> The saying is trustworthy: If anyone [singular] aspires to the office of overseer [*episkopē,* overseership], he desires a noble task. Therefore an overseer [singular] must be above reproach. (1 Tim. 3:2)

The apostle Peter uses the verbal form of the word *overseer, episkopeō,* to describe the role of the elders:

> So I exhort the elders among you, . . . shepherd the flock of God that is among you, exercising oversight [*episkopountes*]. (1 Peter 5:1–2)

The Elders as Overseers

In his final, face-to-face meeting with the Ephesian elders, Paul reminded them that the Holy Spirit himself placed them in the congregation as "overseers," to shepherd God's blood-bought people:

> Now from Miletus he sent to Ephesus and called the elders [*presbyteroi*] of the church to come to him. And when they came to him, he said to them: . . . "[You elders] pay careful attention to yourselves and to all the flock, in which the Holy Spirit has made you overseers, to care for [literally, to shepherd] the church of God, which he obtained with his own blood." (Acts 20:17–18, 28)

The Greek word Paul uses for *elder* is *presbyteros* (pronounced, pres-BU-ter-os). In the Scriptures cited above, Paul associates the term *overseer* with the elders and the work of shepherding and safeguarding "the church of God." So it is evident that the words *overseer* and *elder* refer to the same group of officials, and Paul uses the two terms interchangeably. Thus, any text that deals with overseers is applicable to any text that deals with elders, and vice versa. So whatever functions are assigned to the elders are also assigned to the overseers, and vice versa (for example, *overseers* in 1 Tim. 3:1–7, and *elders* in 1 Tim. 5:17–25).

There Is a Plurality of Overseers and Elders

The churches in Philippi and Ephesus each had a collective body of official overseers or elders, so Paul uses the plural forms "overseers" and "elders" to describe these officials.[2] However, when he lists the required qualifications for the office he uses the singular form, "overseer." This form, in 1 Timothy 3:2 and Titus 1:7, is called a *generic singular,* which is a singular name representing an entire class or type. In this usage, Paul is not referring to the number of overseers in a church but uses the singular *overseer* to stand for all overseers.[3]

This point is important because some scholars take the singular use of "overseer" in 1 Timothy 3:2 and Titus 1:7 to contend that there was only one overseer per house church, and that all

> *Any text that deals with overseers is applicable to any text that deals with elders, and vice versa.*

the individual overseers from the various house churches of a city made up the plurality of elders within that city. But this theory does not agree with the overall New Testament teaching on pastoral oversight of a single church by the plurality of elders.[4]

THE CHURCH OVERSEERS, THE ELDERS

Character and Function

Although the terms *overseer* and *elder* refer to the same official, they are not exactly synonymous terms. Each designation emphasizes different aspects of the office. The term *elder* characterizes the spiritual maturity, experience, wisdom, and character of the individual official. In the Greek translation of the Old Testament, an *elder* was a recognized, mature, community leader. The term *overseer* stresses the ideas of official oversight, guardianship, protection, supervision, and management. Both titles are needed to capture the biblical concepts of what a local church leader is to be in character and function.

When studying any biblical doctrine, it is important to remember that the words, and the original meaning of those words as used by the sacred writers, matter profoundly for a correct understanding of the writers' thinking and teaching. It is not by chance that the New Testament writers avoided terms like "priest," "lord," "ruler," and "king" when describing local church officials. These terms do not fit the unique family nature of the Christian brotherhood and sisterhood or the amazing realities of the Spirit-indwelt body of Christ, the Church. Significantly, the New Testament writers do not emphasize lofty or sacred titles for local church leaders.[5] That occurred later in the centuries to follow.

Different denominations use different terminology to describe their leaders, such as, "pastor," "minister," "preacher," "rector," "bishop," "elder," or "priest." Since this is a biblical study of deacons, we will use the New Testament's own terminology and concepts for those in the official leadership role of the local church.

Because the term *elders* is more commonly used by churches today than the term *overseers*, we will employ the *elder* designation more frequently throughout this book. At times, the words *shepherd* or *pastor* are used to modify the term *elders* in order to clarify that the New Testament Christian concept of elders is pastoral in nature. (The noun *pastor* is the Latin word for *shepherd* and is used commonly to designate local church officials.) Although the elders are not titled *shepherds* (or *pastors*) in the New Testament,[6] they are the ones charged by Scripture to shepherd God's flock. Therefore they are shepherds/pastors.

BIBLICAL ELDERS ARE GOD'S STEWARDS OF GOD'S HOUSEHOLD—THE CHURCH

Titus 1:7 provides a significant insight into the biblical concept of the overseer/elder. In this text, Paul uses the metaphor of a steward to help define the biblical teaching on *overseers* or *elders*:

> Appoint elders in every town as I directed you . . . An overseer, as God's steward, must be above reproach. (Titus 1:5, 7)

Paul uses the Greek term *steward* (*oikonomos*), meaning a household or estate manager, to describe the overseer's position and role in "the household of God" (1 Tim. 3:15). In the ancient world, the household steward, or estate manager, had a great deal of authority over household operations and those who served in the household. Even so, the steward was under the authority of the master, the owner of the house or estate. Anthony C. Thiselton explains:

> This office normally included responsibility for overseeing a household budget, purchasing, accounts, resource allocation, collection of debts, and general running of the establishment, but only as instructed within guidelines agreed by the employer or the head of the house.[7]

The steward's job was to free the master from daily household responsibilities and management so that the master could attend to other matters. To do the job well, the steward had to be a competent manager and completely trustworthy. Here in our passage, the emphasis is on the overseers as *God's* stewards.

The Role and Qualifications of God's Steward

The fact that the overseer/elder is God's steward is highly significant. God appoints the elders to the role of steward and delegates to each of them the authority to manage his household—the church.[8] This is a highly responsible position and role. The steward's authority comes from God, not from the church. God will hold the elders accountable for their service as his stewards.

Just as a household steward in Paul's day was charged with managing funds and people, God's steward must manage church resources, plan budgets, delegate tasks to others, encourage use of members' gifts, solve problems, make decisions, establish church policies, set up structures to accomplish specific work, and lead in one or more ministries of the church. Moreover, he must carefully teach the Word, judge issues and doctrines, provide counsel and education, resolve conflict among members, and care for those in the church household who cannot care for themselves.

Because the elders are God's stewards of God's household, they must meet God's requirements, which Paul delineates in 1 Timothy 3:1–7 and Titus 1:5–9. An elder must be above reproach, the husband of one wife, sober-minded, self-controlled, respectable, hospitable, gentle, a lover of good, upright, holy, disciplined, a good manager of his household, and well thought of by outsiders. He also cannot be arrogant, quick-tempered, violent, quarrelsome, a drunkard, a lover of money, or a recent convert. God's steward must have the ability to educate God's people in sound doctrine, and to refute those who contradict sound doctrine.[9]

One crucial measurement for evaluating one's ability to be God's steward of God's household is the capable management of one's own individual household. The critical importance of this requirement is emphasized by Paul's rhetorical question in 1 Timothy 3:5: "For if someone does not know how to manage his own household, how will he care for God's church?" The answer to that question is a resounding negative—he cannot competently "care for God's church" if he cannot competently manage his own household.

The Greek word rendered "care for" (*epimeleomai*)[10] conveys the idea of diligent, personal attention, and in this case, looking after the various needs of "God's church." As biblical commentator Andreas Köstenberger points out, the phrase "'*God's* church' underscores the sacredness and solemn responsibility of caring for God's people."[11]

God appoints the elders to the role of steward and delegates to each of them the authority to manage his household— the church. . . . The steward's authority comes from God, not from the church. God will hold the elders accountable for their service as his stewards.

BIBLICAL ELDERS ARE TO SHEPHERD GOD'S FLOCK

Consider again Paul's prophetic, apostolic warning to the Ephesian elders. Before he left them, Paul urged them:

> Pay careful attention to yourselves and to all the flock, in which the Holy Spirit has made you overseers, to care for [to shepherd] the church of God, which he obtained with his own blood. I know that after my departure fierce wolves will come in among you, not sparing the flock; and from among your own selves will arise men speaking twisted things, to draw away the disciples after them. Therefore be alert, remembering that for three years I did not cease night or day to admonish everyone with tears. (Acts 20:28–31)

I cannot emphasize enough the theological and practical importance of this apostolic charge to our understanding of the role of the New Testament elders. We would be seriously mistaken to approach this passage theoretically, looking for theological niceties, debating over the accuracy of Luke's reporting, or finding only problems with the passage. Paul's message is crystal clear, solemn, and a matter of life and death to all churches: Guard God's blood-bought flock because savage wolves are coming! This charge reveals Paul's high view of church elders and their work.

Paul pointedly reminded the elders that the Holy Spirit set them in the church as *overseers*. Their specific purpose was "to shepherd the church of God" (literally translated). The particular aspect of the shepherding task Paul stressed here is the protection and guarding of the flock. The flock must be protected from sheep-devouring wolves, so shepherd elders must "be alert" to the ever-present danger of these "fierce wolves." These "fierce wolves" are the agents of Satan, the evil one, enemy, liar, deceiver, tempter, and serpent.[12] The term *overseer* aptly describes their responsibility to guard the flock of God and to be actively alert to imminent and certain danger.

Peter's Charge to the Elders

Not only does Paul use the beautiful, biblical shepherding imagery for the elders, the apostle Peter does the same. He too requires the elders to shepherd God's flock. Peter gives the same charge to numerous churches located "in Pontus, Galatia, Cappadocia, Asia, and Bithynia" (1 Peter 1:1):

> So I exhort the elders among you . . . shepherd the flock of God that is among you, exercising oversight. (1 Peter 5:1–2)

Shepherd is the figurative term that expresses the nature of biblical governance, while *oversee* is the literal term that clarifies the first.

Peter uses the verbs *shepherd* and *oversee* to describe the God-given responsibilities of the elders.

Please note that Peter never mentioned a single overseer, only "the elders." For Peter, who was writing around the same time that Paul wrote 1 Timothy and Titus, the elders are the ones "exercising oversight" of "the flock of God." Since these two preeminent New Testament apostles charge the elders—and no other person or group—to shepherd (or in more contemporary terms, "pastor") the flock of God, we can conclude that, in biblical terms, the elders are responsible for the pastoral oversight of the local church.

BIBLICAL ELDERS ARE TO TEACH
AND DEFEND THE GOSPEL

Titus 1:9 is one of the most important verses for defining Paul's concept of elders/overseers. It requires that all biblical elders be able to teach the Word and to refute false teachers. Thus pastor elders are the guardians and transmitters of the apostles' teaching: "the trustworthy word [the gospel] as taught [by the apostles]."

> [An overseer/elder] must hold firm to the trustworthy word as taught, so that he may be able to give instruction in sound doctrine and also to rebuke those who contradict it. (Titus 1:9)

This passage points out an important difference between the elder and the deacon. An elder must have the ability to teach and defend sound doctrine, which is not required of the deacon.

Some Elders Labor at Preaching and Teaching

Although Scripture requires that all elders be able to teach and defend the truth of the gospel, some elders are Spirit-gifted leaders and some are Spirit-gifted teachers who "*labor* in preaching and teaching." For such strenuous labor, Spirit-gifted teaching elders are properly entitled to receive "double honor" from the congregation. Paul explains this as wages deserved:

> Let the elders who rule well be considered worthy of double honor, especially those who labor in preaching and teaching. For the Scripture says, "You shall not muzzle an ox when it treads out the grain," and "The laborer deserves his wages." (1 Tim. 5:17–18)

These Spirit-gifted teachers are almost certainly the Christ-given "shepherds" (*poimenes*) Paul mentions in Ephesians 4:11, who, along with other teachers, are "to equip the saints for the

An elder must have the ability to teach and defend sound doctrine, which is not required of the deacon.

work of ministry, for building up the body of Christ" (Eph. 4:12). God's plan is that these elders and other teachers perform the critical role of educating God's people to prepare them for their ministry in the body of Christ.

BIBLICAL ELDERS CARE FOR THE WEAK

Paul concludes his plea to the Ephesian elders by focusing on a different aspect of the shepherding task. He makes an appeal to "help the weak":

> In all things I have shown you that by working hard in this way we must help the weak and remember the words of the Lord Jesus, how he himself said, "It is more blessed to give than to receive." (Acts 20:35)

"The weak" are those who cannot secure basic physical and material necessities[13] due to age, sickness, disability, poverty, social status, or any other legitimate reason. So Paul is not referring to spiritually weak Christians, but to those who need financial, medical, or personal assistance. By using the words "we must," and also quoting the Lord Jesus, Paul established as part of the elders' shepherding mandate a biblical and moral obligation to ensure that the "weak" members of God's flock receive proper care.

Paul established as part of the elders' shepherding mandate a biblical and moral obligation to ensure that the "weak" members of God's flock receive proper care.

Examples of Generosity and Care

Biblical elders are to be role models of hard work and big-hearted generosity. By his own example, Paul set the right moral and spiritual tone for the church:

> You yourselves know that these hands ministered to my necessities and to those who were with me. In all things I have shown you that by working hard in this way we must help the weak. (Acts 20:34–35)

Most of the elders Paul spoke to in Acts 20 would have had to provide for their own material needs through some type of employment. Few would have been fully or partly supported by a church body. So Paul cited his own example of self-employment, sacrificial giving, and concern for the weak for the Ephesian elders to imitate. With the money earned from their employment, the elders were to share with those who needed financial assistance.

SUMMARY

A biblical eldership is not a passive, ineffective, uninvolved committee, but a Spirit-appointed body of qualified, functioning shepherds who jointly pastor God's flock. In biblical terms, the elders are the overseers, shepherds, stewards, teachers, and leaders of the local church. They are men who desire to care for God's church and who are above reproach in character, knowledgeable in Scripture, sound in doctrine, able to teach the Word and to protect the church from false teachers. This responsibility gives new life to Paul's commendation that, "If anyone aspires to the office of overseer, he desires a noble task" (1 Tim. 3:1).

In light of these teachings on biblical elders, we are now ready to investigate the New Testament deacons: Who are they? What do they do? What is their relationship to the elders?

Key Points to Remember:

1. For biblically grounded Christians, the role of elders or overseers is defined by the New Testament's distinctive teaching.

2. The terms *overseer* and *elder,* while not synonymous, refer to the same group of officials, and are used interchangeably by Paul as he describes their functions, character, qualifications, and role.

3. As God's stewards, the elders have been entrusted with the responsibility and authority to manage "the household of God," a serious undertaking for which they will be held accountable by their Master.

4. The apostles Paul and Peter charge the elders to pastor and oversee the local church. Deacons are never given such a charge.

5. As part of their shepherding obligation, the elders must care for the "weak" members of God's family.

The Responsibilities of Biblical Elders, the Overseers

- Lead the church of God (1 Tim. 5:17)
- Exercise oversight: manage, supervise (1 Peter 5:2)
- Teach the people God's Word (1 Tim. 3:2; 2 Tim. 2:2; Titus 1:9)
- Equip and prepare the saints for Christian ministry (Eph. 4:11–12)
- Labor in preaching and teaching (1 Tim. 5:17)
- Model Christian leadership (1 Peter 5:3)
- Shepherd, that is, pastor the whole church (1 Peter 5:2): feed, protect, lead, and heal (Acts 20:28)
- Judge doctrinal disputes (Acts 15:2–30; 16:4; 21:20–25)
- Guard the church from false teachers (Acts 20:28–31; Titus 1:9–10)
- Care for the church of God (1 Tim. 3:5)
- Help those within the church who are weak (Acts 20:35)
- Pray for the sick and anoint them with oil (James 5:14–15)
- Lay hands on certain gifted individuals (1 Tim. 4:14)
- Handle church finances (Acts 11:29–30; 1 Peter 5:2)
- Represent their local church to other churches (Acts 11:30; 15:4, 22–23; 21:18–19)
- Held accountable by God the Father (Heb. 13:17)

---

[1]"Now these Jews were more noble than those in Thessalonica; they received the word with all eagerness, examining the Scriptures daily to see if these things were so" (Acts 17:11).
[2]Acts 20:17, 28; Phil. 1:1; 1 Tim. 4:14; 5:17.

[3]Paul freely uses the generic singular *woman, widow, elder*, and *the Lord's servant* when referring to special classes of people (1 Tim. 2:11–14; 5:5, 19; 2 Tim. 2:24). The only occasions that Paul uses *overseer* in the singular are in his lists of qualifications for the office (1 Tim. 3:2; Titus 1:7). In both cases, *overseer* is preceded by the singular construction, "if anyone" (1 Tim. 3:1; Titus 1:6). When he addresses the overseers directly, however, he uses the plural form, because he is addressing a council of overseers, not a single overseer (Phil. 1:1; Acts 20:28).

[4]Acts 14:23; 20:17, 28; Phil. 1:1; 1 Tim. 4:14; James 5:14–15; 1 Peter 5:1–5. See also Benjamin L. Merkle, *The Elder and Overseer: One Office in the Early Church*, Studies in Biblical Literature (New York: Peter Lang, 2003).

[5]Matthew 23:8–12:

> But you are not to be called rabbi, for you have one teacher, and you are all brothers. And call no man your father on earth, for you have one Father, who is in heaven. Neither be called instructors, for you have one instructor, the Christ. The greatest among you shall be your servant. Whoever exalts himself will be humbled, and whoever humbles himself will be exalted.

[6]Ephesians 4:11 refers to Spirit-gifted shepherds: "And he gave the apostles, the prophets, the evangelists, the shepherds and teachers." Here Paul is speaking of Spirit-gifted persons, not the office of overseer/elder. Not all Spirit-gifted shepherds have to be elders. The eldership is a shepherding body, but some elders, not all, are Spirit-gifted shepherds (1 Tim. 5:17). Beginning with the 2007 text edition, the ESV translates with the English word *shepherds* in Ephesians 4:11, rather than *pastors* as in the 2001 edition.

[7]*The First Epistle to the Corinthians: A Commentary on the Greek Text*, NIGTC (Grand Rapids: Eerdmans, 2000), 336; also Ceslas Spicq, *TLNT*, 2: 568–75.

[8]Similarly, according to Acts 20:28, the individual elders sitting before Paul had been placed as overseers in the church by the Holy Spirit.

[9]Titus 1:5–9.

[10]See Celas Spicq, *TLNT*, 2: 47–53.

[11]*Commentary on 1–2 Timothy & Titus*, Biblical Theology for Christian Proclamation (Nashville, TN: B&H, 2017), 130.

[12]Matt. 13:19, 39; John 8:44; 2 Cor. 11:3, 14–15; 1 Thess. 3:5; Rev. 12:9.

[13]"Weak" (*astheneō*): "to experience lack of material necessities, be in need" (*BDAG*, 142).

Chapter 3

DEACONS, ASSISTANTS TO THE ELDERS

Now that we have examined the biblical teaching regarding the church's overseers, we can better understand Paul's concept of deacons.

A critical factor in our study is the use of the Greek word *diakonos* in Philippians 1:1, 1 Timothy 3:8–12, and a possible, but debated, use in Romans 16:1. Of the twenty-one occurrences of *diakonos* in Paul's letters, the *English Standard Version* transliterates only three of them as "deacons" (Phil. 1:1; 1 Tim. 3:8, 12). In these texts Paul uses *diakonoi* (plural) in reference to certain local church officials who are associated with the overseers.

Furthermore, Paul uses the term in a positive, honorable sense, not in a way that implies servile labor. I have heard claims that the term *diakonos* means a lowly servant who dusts tables, implying that deacons do the most menial jobs in the church, like cleaning bathrooms and mopping floors. This is clearly not the case in both Philippians 1:1 and 1 Timothy 3:8–13, the principal texts that address deacons. In these passages, deacons clearly occupy a position of recognized authority and lead in certain official duties. In fact, Paul states that those who serve well will gain for themselves the esteem and respect of the congregation (1 Tim. 3:13).

In both texts, Paul links the deacons with the church overseers. Overseers as well as deacons are acknowledged church officials who have been examined and approved by the church and its leaders as scripturally qualified for their respective offices. The officeholders designated as *overseers* (*episkopoi*) have oversight of the whole church (Acts 20:28; Titus 1:7), so it is significant that deacons are mentioned alongside them and that Paul places deacons *after* the overseers in the order of mention.

Clearly the church officeholders Paul designated as *diakonoi* serve under the overseers' leadership. But what do we know about the relationship between the overseers and deacons and the ways in which the deacons serve? In this chapter I will seek to show that the deacons are the formal assistants to the elders. Although a number of scholars affirm this view,[1] they rarely present evidence to support this position. In this chapter, I present linguistic and contextual evidence that the *diakonoi* are the assistants to the *episkopoi* (overseers).

EVIDENCE FOR DEACONS AS ASSISTANTS

The claim that the deacons are the assistants to the overseers/elders is based on the following arguments. Remember that the Bereans carefully examined the great apostle Paul's claims to see if they agreed with Holy Scripture. That took time and effort. I encourage you to do the same with the arguments presented in this chapter.

1. *Assistant*, One Possible Meaning of *Diakonos*

In recent years, scholars have shown that there is a wider linguistic range of meaning of the *diakon-* word group than previously acknowledged. This word group can extend in meaning from a sacred, divinely commissioned messenger (that is, an ambassador or emissary),[2] to a lowly, slave-like table waiter or household servant, or even to an authorized official with authority to carry out the command of a superior.[3] So not every use of *diakonos* means simply "servant" or carries menial, servile connotations. Therefore, we must interpret *diakonos* and its corresponding terms *diakoneō* and *diakonia* within the specific contexts in which they are used.

As part of his doctoral dissertation, Clarence D. Agan III completed an extensive lexical study of the *diakon-* word group (*diakoneō, diakonia, diakonos*).[4] He examined 770 uses of the word group from secular, Jewish, and Christian sources dating from the sixth century BC to the early third century AD. To date, Agan's study is the most comprehensive and examines the largest number of occurrences of the *diakon-* word group.

As a result of his research, Agan proposes four uses of the *diakon-* word group:

(1) Table attendance: a waiter, server, attendant, with the duties of serving food and drink, waiting on tables, meal service, or preparation of a meal (Luke 17:8; John 2:9).[5] This usage of the *diakon-* word group is the most familiar to Christians.

(2) Domestic attendance: a domestic servant or slave with the function of performing a wide range of household activities or attending to the personal needs of the master (Matt. 25:44; John 12:26).

(3) Communication or delivery: an officially commissioned messenger, emissary, or courier who delivers a message or an item on behalf of another (Rom. 16:1; 2 Cor. 3:3; Eph. 3:7–9).[6]

(4) Agency or instrumentality: one who carries out the will of another, or a task on behalf of another. In many contexts, the idea is that of a subordinate carrying out an assignment on a superior's behalf and having full authority to execute the

superior's delegated task (Acts 19:22; Rom. 13:4;[7] 2 Cor. 11:15).[8] This is the least frequent usage of the term and often is found in verb forms.[9]

Based on his assessment, Clarence Agan concludes that *diakonos* in 1 Timothy 3 and Philippians 1 expresses "agency," rather than "table waiting" (as is possibly suggested by the table-serving ministry for the poor in Acts 6:1–7). The point that is particularly relevant to our investigation is that Agan demonstrates that one of the possible meanings of the *diakon-* word group is "agency."* The deacons, he maintains, are the church-approved assistants or aides to the elders.

Of note, the third edition of *A Greek-English Lexicon of the New Testament and Other Early Christian Literature* (abbreviated as *BDAG*), following more recent research on the *diakon-* word group,[10] lists one entry for the Greek word *diakonos* as: "one who gets something done, at the behest of a superior, *assistant to someone*."[11] The entries for *diakonos* as it appears in Philippians 1:1 and 1 Timothy 3:8, 12 are *"attendant, assistant, aide."*[12]

In recent years scholars have shown that there is a wider linguistic range of meaning of the diakon- *word group than previously acknowledged.*

---

2. Eliminating Alternative Usages of *Diakonos*

Let us now consider and eliminate other possible usages of the word *diakonos* that do not fit the 1 Timothy 3:1–13 context.

First, Paul obviously does not use *diakonos* in 1 Timothy

---

*To view examples of the *diakon-* word group used for agency in extrabiblical literature, see www.deaconbook.com.

3:8 to mean a commissioned messenger or envoy (the third use of the term). There is nothing in the text of 1 Timothy 3:1–13 that indicates travel, message-bearing, or service as a special envoy or a missionary.

Second, Paul is not using the term *diakonos* to mean a servant in a general, undefined sense that could apply to any Christian (the second use of the term, metaphorically applied). Some churches hold that anyone who regularly serves in the church in any capacity is a deacon (= servant). They make this claim on the assumption that *diakonos* can mean *servant* and nothing more.

However, biblical scholars almost universally reject this view.[13] Most church leaders sense the problems inherent in the idea that anyone who serves in the church is a deacon. They correctly understand that *diakonoi* in 1 Timothy 3 and Philippians 1 refers to a limited number of church officeholders, not to every person in the church who serves.

Agency or instrumentality: one who carries out the will of another, or a task on behalf of another. In many contexts, the idea is that of a subordinate carrying out an assignment on a superior's behalf and having full authority to execute the superior's delegated task.

Third, although many scholars reject the idea that all who serve in the church are deacons, they still believe that *diakonos* in 1 Timothy 3 must mean *servant* and nothing more. They identify these servants in different ways, e.g., "gifted servants," "model servants," or "leading servants." In this view, it appears that the term *diakonos* (= servant) is a title given to various people in the church for doing different kinds of service, for example, "assisting with parking,"[14] directing the church's audio-visual ministry, coordinating weddings, or leading the greeting-ushering ministry of the church. The position/office of deacon does not appear to be a specific office with a clear identity one is admitted to, but rather a title given to people leading diverse ministries within the church. This view, however, is built on a faulty lexical assumption that the word *diakonos* must mean *servant* and cannot mean anything else.

Fourth, there is no clear indication in the context of 1 Timothy 3:1–13 that the term *diakonos* is being used as a specialized title for table-serving officials who feed the poor (the first usage).[15] No contextual markers suggest anything to do with food, table service, or the needy. At best this is an inference. A better understanding of *diakonos* is derived from its close association with the overseers (1 Tim. 3:1–7), and its subordinate position to them.

3. The Deacons' Association with the Position and Authority of the Overseers

The key to understanding the deacons of 1 Timothy 3:8–13 is to accurately understand the officials with whom they are associated: that is, the overseer, superintendent, supervisor, or guardian (see Chapter 2). The position and work of the overseer is referred to as "the office of overseer" (v. 1), which Paul emphasizes is "a noble task" (v. 1). Paul requires that the overseer be able to teach God's Word and to care for God's church as a "steward" of God's household (1 Tim. 3:2, 5; Titus 1:7, 9).

Because of their prominent position and critical role in the church, Paul delineates a list of qualifications for overseers that is more comprehensive than those for deacons (1 Tim. 3:2–7). According to the information we have from the New Testament, overseers/elders were appointed first before deacons. Churches must have qualified overseers/elders, but they do not require deacons (as in Titus 1:5–10). The overseers do not need the deacons in order to function as the overseers or stewards of the local church, as will be explained in detail below.

The Right Word for the Job: In the same context (1 Tim. 3:1–13), Paul addresses another body of church officials (termed *diakonoi*) who are paired with and subordinate to the overseers but are *not* required to be able to teach and are *not* given a specific list of responsibilities. Therefore, it seems most likely that the officials called *diakonoi* are in fact aides or assistants of the overseer. They are designated *diakonoi* precisely because of their relationship with the *episkopoi*.[16]

As John N. Collins concludes, the *episkopoi* can stand alone, but the deacons must stand in relationship to someone or some body for direction:

> From the nature of the terms, *episkopoi* could operate without *diakonoi*, but *diakonoi* could not operate without some such mandating functionary as an *episkopos*.[17]

Thus, the deacons are not a separate, autonomous body of officials disconnected from the body of overseers. As the context and the terms themselves indicate, the *diakonoi* operate under the

They are designated diakonoi precisely because of their relationship with the episkopoi.

leadership of the *episkopoi*. The *diakonoi* assist the *episkopoi* by officially representing the overseers and standing ready to carry out tasks delegated by the overseers.

Paul most likely chose the particular Greek word *diakonos* because, as Clarence Agan succinctly explains, the term:

> better captures the intermediary function Paul had in mind. He was thinking of a role that involved being simultaneously

in-and-under authority—under the authority of the elders, but having authority over the congregation to carry out tasks as needed. *Diakonos* provided a clear way to say this while still leaving room for flexibility as to the nature of the specific tasks deacons might undertake.[18]

As you can see, the view that *diakonos* means *assistant* is built on more objective linguistic and contextual evidence than the undefined, leading-servant or table-serving views.

Overseer-Deacon Relationship: Scholars have speculated a good deal about the relationship between deacons and overseers. Translating the Greek word *diakonos* as *assistant* explains at once the relationship between the two groups, *episkopoi* and *diakonoi*.

The relationship between the overseers and the assistants should not be mistakenly viewed as one of master-servant. The overseers are not the deacons' masters, and the deacons are not the domestic servants of the elders, serving their every personal whim, want, or need. But if *diakonos* means assistant of the overseer in his official capacity, this would explain nicely why the term *diakonos* was used and accurately conveys the relationship between the two offices.

The deacons represent the overseers/elders and act on their behalf in service to God's church. It follows, then, that they, like the elders, need to be properly qualified, examined, and approved by the church. And, as assistants of the elders and church officeholders, the deacons will exercise a measure of formal authority in the congregation, but always under the authority of the elders.

4. A Simple Translation and Explanation

The title "assistants" describes instantly who the deacons are and what they do without elaborate explanation or assumptions that are not biblically provable, e.g., "exemplary servants," "leading servants," or "table servants."

The assistants-to-the-overseers view answers most questions about the role of the deacons, not in detail, but in general terms that can be adapted by any local church eldership. Otherwise, it is hard to explain the use of *diakonoi* for local church officials, or what they do, or how they relate to the overseers. The simplicity of this interpretation of *diakonos* is a very strong argument in its favor.

***Diakonoi* as Assistants:** A few English Bible translations render *diakonoi* in the two deacon passages as "assistants."[19] For example, the distinguished Greek scholar, Edgar Goodspeed, in *The New Testament: An American Translation*, renders *diakonoi* as "assistants" in both passages. His translation instantly communicates who the *diakonoi* are and generally what they do:

> Paul and Timothy, slaves of Christ Jesus, to all the devoted adherents of Christ Jesus who are in Philippi, with the superintendents and assistants. (Phil. 1:1)

> Assistants, in turn, must be serious, straightforward men, not addicted to wine or dishonest gain. . . . The assistants must be only once married,[20] and manage their children and their households well. For those who do good service as assistants gain a good standing for themselves and great confidence in their faith in Christ Jesus. (1 Tim. 3:8, 12–13)

Deacons or Assistants? The English term *deacon*, like the term *apostle* (*emissary*), which is also a transliteration of the Greek *apostolos*, is such a familiar part of our specialized church vocabulary that we will continue to employ it in this book. Most times we will render *diakonoi* as *deacons*, and sometimes we will translate *diakonoi* as *assistants* in our two principal passages. We will always render *apostoloi* as *apostles*, not emissaries (or envoys, messengers), although that is a correct translation, but unfamiliar to us. We do not say the "twelve emissaries" or the "twelve messengers" (although correct), but the twelve apostles. Thus we will most times use the familiar transliteration *deacons* for *diakonoi*.

5. The Need for Official Assistants

Paul himself required assistants to help him in his gospel mission. Luke records that Timothy and Erastus served Paul as "helpers" or "assistants":

> And having sent into Macedonia two of his helpers [*diakonountōn autō*, "those who assisted him"], Timothy and Erastus, [Paul] himself stayed in Asia for a while. (Acts 19:22)

A number of commentators and English translations render the Greek verb form of *diakonos* here as "assistants."[21] From his own experience of having assistants and caring for churches, Paul would know of the elders' need for formal assistants.

The New Testament emphasizes the strenuous labor and toil required of church leaders. Just as the twelve apostles devoted themselves "to prayer and to the ministry of the word" (Acts 6:4), there were in the church at Ephesus elders who devoted themselves to "labor in preaching and teaching" the Word (1 Tim. 5:17). These hard-working elders would profit greatly from having official assistance to help bear the heavy pastoral burdens of their congregation.

Given Paul's unique apostolic authority and strategic church planting ministry, it is quite possible (the Scripture does not say) that he established a formal position in the church to provide qualified assistants to help the elders in their shepherding oversight of God's flock. He is the *only* New Testament writer to mention assistants and to stipulate the qualifications for this office. He had the Christ-given authority to establish a new church office and

DEACONS, ASSISTANTS TO THE ELDERS

choose *diakonoi* as its title. He demonstrated his full endorsement by using the title and by regulating the requisites for the position. There would be no office of deacon if Paul, Christ's apostle and teacher of the churches in Philippi and Ephesus, did not approve of and foster such a position.

Deacons Are Not Elders or Teachers

Finally, I need to point out that some advocates of the assistants-to-the-overseers view misapply this interpretation by removing any meaningful distinction between elders and deacons. For example, in his commentary on the Pastoral Epistles, Philip Towner argues for the deacons' full "participation in the ministry of teaching and preaching."[22] He contends that,

> We should probably understand the deacon's task as being that of assisting the overseer/supervisor in administration, leadership, and teaching within the church. The arrangement in Ephesus was apparently that of a group of deacons (note the plurality) serving the church as assistants either to the overseer (singular) or team of elders.[23]

Commenting on the qualification that the deacon must be able to manage his own household well (v. 12), Towner goes on to say:

> The concern for this management ability suggests that deacons carried out significant leadership duties in service to the overseers, or perhaps (if overseers supervised a cluster of house churches in a locality) on a par with overseers but in a more limited sphere (the house church).[24]

In a similar manner, R. Alastair Campbell suggests that deacons may have been leaders of their own individual house churches under the supervision of an overseer.[25]

But if deacons carry out all the same tasks of the overseers they are, at least in practice, filling the elders/overseers' role. The presence of two similar offices that each provide teaching and governance is a surefire formula for confusion and power struggles, even if the deacons are, in theory, subject to the elders. Paul was a wise master builder (1 Cor. 3:10) who understood human nature and would have known that such an arrangement would be an organizational disaster, a source of conflict and disorder. It is highly unlikely that Paul would establish two offices doing pretty much the same things.

Teaching Not a Requirement

The critical qualification that an overseer/elder "be able to give instruction in sound doctrine and also to rebuke those who contradict it" (Titus 1:9) is *not* required of deacons. This is not an accidental omission on Paul's part. Making deacons teachers and preachers does not agree with Paul's listing of their requisite qualifications and only confuses matters. Paul's omission of this requirement must be taken seriously if we are to understand his doctrine of deacons.

Scholars who hold the view that deacons are to teach like elders do cite the qualification to "hold the mystery of the faith with a clear conscience" (1 Tim. 3:9), as an indication that deacons are to conduct such teaching and preaching.[26] But this interpretation is unsupported by Scripture, as will be explained in Chapter 5.

To clarify, the "clear conscience" requirement addresses the candidate's lifestyle. A deacon cannot be a hypocrite. His life, doctrine, belief and practice, must match or be lived "with a clear conscience." Those who equate deacons with Bible study leaders, teachers, or evangelists, are only generating more confusion about deacons.

Summary

The view that deacons are the official assistants of the elders has much to commend it. Since Paul never explicitly explained who the deacons are or what they do, we must settle on the interpretation that offers the best supporting factual evidence with the least amount of difficulty.

I have concluded that the assistants-to-the-overseers view is the best interpretation because it provides the most objective evidence both lexically and contextually with the least amount of guesswork involved. Furthermore, I am persuaded that the assistant-to-the-overseers view is the best option because the alternative views are unsatisfactory, demand too much guesswork, and cannot ultimately be proven contextually or lexically. So much of what I hear and read about deacons is based on mere assertion rather than evidence or argumentation.

In the next chapter, we will consider more closely what assistants to the elders would do to aid the elders and free them to stay focused on feeding and protecting the flock of God.

Key Points to Remember:

1. The four uses of the *diakon-* word group:

   (1) Table attendance
   (2) Domestic attendance
   (3) Communication and delivery
   (4) Agency and instrumentality

2. Of the four uses of the *diakon-* word group, the idea of agency best fits the *diakonoi* of 1 Timothy 3:8–13. Deacons are the qualified, approved assistants to the elders.

3. The translation of *diakonoi* as "assistants" describes who the deacons are and what they do without elaborate explanation or assumptions that are not biblically provable, e.g., "leading servants." The simplicity of this interpretation of *diakonos* is a very strong argument in its favor.

4. The ability to teach the Word, required of the elder, is a distinguishing feature that sets the overseeing elders apart from the deacons.

5. Since Paul does not explicitly say who the deacons are, we must settle on the interpretation that incorporates the best supporting evidence and presents the least amount of difficulty. The assistant-to-the-elders position is the best interpretation.

---

[1]Advocates of this view: Hermann Cremer, *Biblio-Theological Lexicon of New Testament Greek,* 4th ed. (Edinburgh: T&T Clark, 1895), 178; Walter Lock, *The Pastoral Epistles,* ICC (Edinburgh: T&T Clark, 1924), 34–35; E. F. Scott, *The Pastoral Epistles,* MNTC (London: Hodder and Stoughton, 1936), 34; R. C. H Lenski, *The Interpretation of St. Paul's Epistles to the Colossians, to the Thessalonians, to Timothy, to Titus and to Philemon* (Minneapolis, MN: Augsburg, 1937), 592; E. K. Simpson, *The Pastoral Epistles* (Grand Rapids: 1954), 55; Eduard Schweizer, *Church Order in the New Testament* (Naperville, IL: Allenson, 1961), 199; J. N. D. Kelly, *The Pastoral Epistles: I Timothy, II Timothy, Titus,* BNTC (London: Adam & Charles Black, 1963), 81; Gerald F. Hawthorne, *Philippians,* WBC (Waco, TX: Word, 1983), 9 (a possible interpretation); Thomas C. Oden, *First and Second Timothy and Titus: Interpretation* (Louisville, KY: John Knox, 1989), 147; John N. Collins, *Diakonia: Reinterpreting the Ancient Sources* (New York: Oxford University Press, 1990), 237, 243, 337; R. Alastair Campbell, *The Elders: Seniority within Earliest Christianity* (Edinburgh: T&T Clark, 1994), 134, 199–200; Daniel Arichea and Howard Hatton, *Handbook on Paul's Letters to Timothy and to Titus* (New York: United Bible Society, 1995), 72; *The Oxford Dictionary of the Christian Church*, ed. F. A. Cross (New York: Oxford Press, 1998), 455; *BDAG*, "diakonos" [2000], 230–31, [This lexicon is abbreviated as *BDAG* for Bauer-Danker-Arndt-Gingrich. This is the 3rd edition]; Philip H. Towner, *The Letters to Timothy and Titus,* NICNT (Grand Rapids: Eerdmans, 2006), 262, 267; Benjamin Fiore, *Sacra Pagina: The Pastoral Epistles* (Collegeville, MN: Liturgical, 2007), 80–82; Paul Trebilco,

The Early Christians in Ephesus from Paul to Ignatius (Grand Rapids: Eerdmans, 2007), 458–59, 523 (a possible interpretation); Carolyn Osiek, "Deacon," in *The New Interpreter's Dictionary of the Bible*, vol. 2, ed. Katharine D. Sakenfeld, (Nashville, TN: Abingdon, 2007), 2: 49; Joseph H. Hellerman, *Philippians*, EGGNT (Nashville, TN: B&H Academic, 2015), 12.

[2]Collins, *Diakonia*, 96–132.

[3]Collins, *Diakonia*, 133–49. See Josephus, *Jewish Antiquities* 9.25.

[4]"Like the One Who Serves: Jesus, Servant-Likeness, and Self-Humiliation in the Gospel of Luke," PhD dissertation (University of Aberdeen, 1999). Also, Clarence D. Agan, III, "Deacons, Deaconesses, and Denominational Discussions: Romans 16:1 as a Test Case," *Presbyterion: Covenant Seminary Review*, 34/2 (Fall 2008), 105–08.

Agan follows, but not uncritically, John Collins's ground-breaking book, *Diakonia: Re-interpreting the Ancient Sources* (op. cit.). He seeks to correct some of Collin's imbalances and overcorrections. Also critical of some of Collins's specific applications to New Testament texts is Andrew Clarke, *Serve the Community of the Church: Christians as Leaders and Ministers* (Grand Rapids: Eerdmans, 2000), 234–47; and *A Pauline Theology of Church Leadership* (New York: Bloomsbury, 2008), 60–67. Agreement with Collins's view of deacons as assistants to the overseers should not be taken to mean an endorsement of all his conclusions or interpretations, some of which are quite erroneous, i.e., Acts 6:1–7, Mark 10:45 (see *Deacons and the Church*, 28–35, 58).

[5]John Collins states that, "In the case of this word group, it is true that a reference to service at table is the most common single reference," occurring "in about a quarter of all instances" (*Diakonia*, 75).

[6]Dieter Georgi draws on his own original research of the ancient *diakon-* word group and the sacred commissioned messenger aspect of *diakonos*. He claims that deacons are heralds and proclaimers of the gospel, never ministers of charity; they are the missionaries or evangelists of the church (*The Opponents of Paul in Second Corinthians* [Philadelphia: Fortress, 1986], 27–32). He has not won many supporters to his opinion that deacons are missionaries, preachers, or evangelists.

[7]*BDAG*, 230.

[8]These are some key examples of Agan's list of non-biblical, Hellenistic usages of *diakon-* terminology meaning *agency*:

Verb forms:

Josephus, *Jewish Antiquities* 9.25, 41; 18.269, 283; 19.42.

Appian, *Roman History* 3.12.2; 12.13.90.

Aristides, *To Plato in Defense of the Four* 196, 230, 265, 367, 556.

Noun form:

Josephus, *Jewish Antiquities* 11.255; *Jewish War* 4.388.

Dio Chrysostom, *Discourses* 49.8.

Philo, *De Decalogo* 177.

Philo, *De Gigantibus* 12.

Philo, *De Specialibus Legibus* 1.116.

Philo, *De Josepho* 123, 242.
Aristides, *To Plato in Defense of Oratory* 225, 364, 367.
Aristides, *To Plato in Defense of the Four* 266, 590.
Aristides of Athens, *Apology* 15.

[9]Collins remarks: "So far as the common noun is concerned, the notion of agency is not widely represented in the Christian usage of the period" (*Diakonia*, 243, 331). Agan states:

> Yet in this final semantic domain our terms are at their most abstract, designating simply the effecting of another's will by an agent (if personal), or instrument (if impersonal), without reference to food and drink, to household duties, or to messages or objects to be delivered ("Deacons, Deaconesses, and Denominational Discussions: Romans 16:1 as a Test Case," 101–02).

[10]Compare the entries for the *diakon-* terms of the previous edition (1979) of *BDAG* with the third edition (2000) for the acknowledgment of a broader range of meaning.

[11]*BDAG*, 230–31; see also page 919.

[12]*BDAG*, 230–31.

[13]There are scriptural requirements to be met before one can serve as a deacon or be called a deacon. Such conditions limit the number of people who can serve in the church as deacons. Yet, even those who do not meet all the deacon qualifications are still required by Christ to do "the work of ministry [or service]" (Eph. 4:12). The view that everyone who serves the church is a deacon washes away any credible distinction between officers with the title "deacon" and all non-titled servants who are also obligated to serve in many different ways.

[14]According to this view, deacons are leaders or coordinators over various ministries within and without the local church, e.g., "leading the parking team":

> The first responsibility of deacons is to meet needs according to the Word. To be clear, some areas of service, such as assisting with parking, may not be specifically mentioned in Scripture, but they fulfill a specific need related to a scriptural mandate. A deacon who leads a parking team enables the church to obey the biblical command to meet together (Heb. 10:24–25) (David Platt, Daniel L. Akin, and Tony Merida, *1 & 2 Timothy and Titus*, CCE [Nashville, TN: Broadman & Holman, 2013], 60).

[15]This is the view I previously held and argued for in my book, *The New Testament Deacon: The Church's Minister of Mercy* (Littleton, CO: Lewis and Roth), 1992). At the time of writing *The New Testament Deacon*, neither John Collins's nor Clarence Agan's research was available. It was particularly Clarence Agan's doctoral dissertation that changed my view.

[16]If the deacons were the assistants of the elders, we might expect Paul to have made that clear by adding "their" before *diakonoi*. Instead, there is no qualifying word or phrase attached to the title *diakonoi*. However, the term *diakonoi* in the specific context of church officeholders, in close association with the *episkopos*, and with the meaning of agency, does not require the possessive pronoun or the definite article. Note that the following persons are referred to anarthrously (without the article) in

1 Timothy 3: deacons, vv. 8, 12; children, vv. 4, 12; wives, vv. 2, 12; husbands, vv. 2, 12; and wives/women, v. 11.

[17]Collins, *Deacons and the Church* (Harrisburg, PA: Morehouse, 2002), 92.

[18]Personal email correspondence with the author, July 7, 2016.

[19]"Overseers and assistants" (Phil. 1:1), in Charles B. Williams, *The New Testament: A Private Translation in the Language of the People* (Chicago: Moody, 1954). "Ministers of the Church and their assistants" (Phil. 1:1) in Richard Francis Weymouth, *The Modern Speech New Testament* (New York: Baker & Taylor, 1902).

[20]Most commentators today reject the translation, "must be only once married" (*mias gynaikos andres*, "the husband of one wife"), in favor of the meaning "marital faithfulness."

[21]Joseph A. Fitzmyer, C. K. Barrett, Eckhard J. Schnabel, Simon J. Kistemaker, REB, NET, NLT, Phillips, Goodspeed; "his 'deacons' or *ministers*" (Richard B. Rackham); "helpers" (NIV, NRSV, GNB). Agan contends, however, that "assistants" is not the correct usage of the term in this context. He proposes that "messengers" or "couriers" better suits the present context of travel and message bearing: "those who serve as representative spokesmen and/or undertake 'missions' or 'errands' on his behalf" ("Deacons, Deaconesses, and Denominational Discussions," 101).

[22]Towner, *The Letters to Timothy and Titus,* 262.

[23]Towner, *The Letters to Timothy and Titus,* 262; see also I. Howard Marshall, *The Pastoral Epistles,* ICC (Edinburgh: T&T Clark, 1999), 487–88; Trebilco, *Early Christians*, 459, 523.

[24]Towner, *The Letters to Timothy and Titus,* 267.

[25]*The Elders*, 199–200.

[26]Marshall, *The Pastoral Epistles*, 487–88; Towner, *The Letters to Timothy and Titus,* 262.

Chapter 4

Assisting the Elders with the Care of God's Church

From the second century to the present day, many Bible scholars and church leaders have thought that the origin of the deacons is recorded in Acts 6. In this passage, the twelve apostles appointed seven officials to care for the church's poor in Jerusalem. Luke records this event in Acts 6:1–7:

> Now in these days when the disciples were increasing in number, a complaint by the Hellenists arose against the Hebrews because their widows were being neglected in the daily distribution.
>
> And the twelve summoned the full number of the disciples and said, "It is not right that we should give up preaching the word of God to serve tables. Therefore, brothers, pick out from among you seven men of good repute, full of the Spirit and of wisdom, whom we will appoint to this duty. But we will devote ourselves to prayer and to the ministry of the word."
>
> And what they said pleased the whole gathering, and they chose Stephen, a man full of faith and of the Holy Spirit, and Philip, and Prochorus, and Nicanor, and Timon, and Parmenas, and Nicolaus, a proselyte of Antioch. These they set before the apostles, and they prayed and laid their hands on them. (Acts 6:1–6)

THE SEVEN OF ACTS 6 AND THE ASSISTANTS OF 1 TIMOTHY 3

The problem with trying to connect the Seven of Acts 6 with the later deacons is that neither Luke nor Paul state such a connection. In fact, Luke assigns no title or designation, such as almoners or table servants, to the Seven. The closest he comes to giving them a name is "the seven" (Acts 21:8). Furthermore, nothing in the 1 Timothy 3:8–13 passage indicates table service or food distribution, which is prominent in the Acts 6 passage. As we have contended, Paul uses *diakonos* in 1 Timothy 3 to identify aides or assistants of the elders, not as a designation for table servants.

> *The problem with trying to connect the Seven of Acts 6 with the later deacons is that neither Luke nor Paul state such a connection.*

The Seven of Acts 6 were specifically chosen by the congregation and appointed by the Twelve for one task only: serving tables. That is, the Seven were to provide charitable relief for the church's many impoverished members (Acts 6:3).[1] But in 1 Timothy 3, Paul assigns no specific tasks for the *diakonoi*/assistants of the elders. As the term *assistants* indicates, the deacons do what the elders assign them to do so as to allow the elders to focus more on feeding, leading, and protecting God's flock.

With that said, one obvious and biblically mandated task with which all church elders need constant assistance is—as Acts 6 unforgettably illustrates—the care of the church's poor and needy.*

---

*For a detailed exposition of Acts 6:1–7, go to www.deaconbook.com.

An Apostolic Precedent

From the Old Testament Scriptures and the teachings of Christ, the apostles and early Christians knew that providing for the poor was not an optional ministry. It was a biblically mandated ministry. Our Lord declared of himself that the Spirit "has anointed me to proclaim good news to the poor" (Luke 4:18). As a result of the preaching of the gospel, many poor people became Christians. Thus, chronic poverty was a major challenge for almost all the churches of the first century.[2]

The beginning of the book of Acts reveals that the twelve apostles originally were responsible for administering the church's charitable aid and for the preaching-teaching ministry of the church. As they soon discovered, ministering the Word *and* serving tables became an overwhelming burden that adversely affected both ministries. The stresses led the Twelve to establish table-serving officials who would manage the benevolence ministry, thereby allowing the apostles to focus on gospel proclamation and teaching the new believers to observe all that Jesus had commanded (Matt. 28:19–20).

What the twelve apostles did and said about the problem of poverty and their Christ-given priorities of prayer and the Word echoed throughout the first churches. Their example was of utmost interest to Paul, the Ephesian elders, and other newly formed churches when they faced the same issues and problems.

The Acts 6 account would have been of particular interest to the church elders (more so than to the deacons) because they were the *closest analogous leadership body to the apostles*.[3] Hence, what the twelve apostles said about their ministry crisis (v. 2) and their God-given priorities (v. 4) would likely have influenced the thinking and practices of early church elders.

In a speech to the first church, presented in the most concise language, the twelve apostles declared their ministry priorities:

> It is not right that we should give up preaching the word of God to serve tables. (Acts 6:2)

> We will devote ourselves to prayer and to the ministry of the word. (Acts 6:4)

The apostles' speech is in one hundred percent agreement with the rest of the New Testament's extraordinary emphasis on preaching "the word of God" and teaching all believers to obey all that Christ commanded. Christianity was and is a preaching-teaching movement. Therefore, the apostles' words are as relevant today as they were on the day they were spoken. Their speech needs to be repeated, memorized, and studied by all pastor elders.

God's Word creates, edifies, protects, strengthens, encourages, and guides the church. The apostles' stated priorities of "prayer" and "the ministry of the word" should be the priorities of all biblical elders.[4] Deacons best assist the elders by helping them to keep their focus on the supreme importance of feeding, guiding, and protecting God's flock by "the word of truth, the gospel of your salvation" (Eph. 1:13).

Charitable Ministry in Jerusalem and Ephesus

There are many similarities between Acts 6:1–7 and the letter of 1 Timothy. This is because both Acts 6 and the letter of 1 Timothy deal directly with the common, but fundamental, ministries of charitable care and the ministry of the Word in the local church. Just as the church in Jerusalem had a structure in place to provide for its dependent widows, the church in Ephesus also had a widows' roll and a mechanism for distributing aid to its widows (1 Tim. 5:3–16). Moreover, the Ephesian church had elders who labored diligently in order to lead and teach the church (1 Tim. 5:17–18).

As providing for the poor is a particularly demanding, relentless, and time-consuming work, it is likely that the Ephesian elders, like the twelve apostles in Jerusalem, needed administrative assistance with the care of the church's widows and other needy people so that they could concentrate more effectively on leading and teaching the church.

Deacons best assist the elders by helping them to keep their focus on the supreme importance of feeding, guiding, and protecting God's flock by "the word of truth, the gospel of your salvation" (Eph. 1:13).

Charitable Ministry in the Post-Apostolic Era

From the post-apostolic literature of the next three centuries, we see that the deacons became closely associated with the church's charitable relief work. They were regularly (but not exclusively) associated with the care of the poor and the sick and the distribution of charitable gifts.[5] In fact, in Rome, "the social task of the deacons appears to be so extensive that subdeacons were assigned to assist them."[6]

By the end of the second century and the beginning of the third, the deacons had become the formal assistants of the bishop (that is, the overseer or minister).[7] They served as the ears and eyes of the overseer. Yet even as official assistants to the overseer, deacons were associated most often with collecting offerings for the poor, reporting to the overseer on the condition of the sick, and meeting practical needs of the church's suffering members.[8]

Even today, deacons in every branch of Christianity are associated in some way with the care of the needy.[9] This long-standing tradition has its roots in the historic practices of the earliest Christians and their local churches.

More Than Table Servers

Paul was in Jerusalem at the time of the appointment of the Seven and was thoroughly familiar with the events of Acts 6. Although he would wholeheartedly agree with what the apostles did, his solution for relieving overburdened elders goes beyond that of the Acts 6 model. Unlike the table-serving officials of Acts 6, Paul's *diakonoi* are not limited to charitable ministries, even if care for the poor and the sick became a major part of their responsibilities, as is likely.

By designating the officials of 1 Timothy 3:8–13 as *assistants* and not table servers, Paul allows them to do other demanding tasks that would assist the elders in the "care for God's church" (1 Tim. 3:5). The help of qualified, approved assistants who have the authority to carry out tasks delegated by the pastor elders relieves the elders of certain demanding tasks and helps them to keep their focus on their primary ministry of leading and feeding God's flock. The designation of such assistants is in keeping with the intent of the table-serving Seven appointed in the church in Jerusalem.

Tasks Determined by the Elders

The specific tasks of the deacons are to be determined by the elders in accordance with the church's particular needs, size, and giftedness of its members. Certainly elders need continuous help with official hospital visits and phone calls, checking on absentees, managing charitable gifts, distributing aid to the needy, assisting families in distress, visiting and protecting the elderly and shut-ins, helping with finances, overseeing church property, and carrying out certain administrative tasks. In a large church, different deacons may be assigned different areas of responsibility based on their spiritual giftedness and interests.

Paul uses the plural form *deacons* in 1 Timothy 3:8, 12,

indicating that he envisioned more than one deacon to assist the elders. As to the number of deacons needed, the elders would have to determine that according to the needs of the church and its elders and the availability of qualified individuals. In some churches, there may be only one person who qualifies for the office. It is better to have one qualified deacon than to have three who do not meet the biblical standards.

The help of qualified, approved assistants . . . relieves the elders of certain demanding tasks and helps them to keep their focus on their primary ministry of leading and feeding God's flock.

First Elders, then Deacons

In his letter to Titus, written about the same time as 1 Timothy, Paul delineated the qualifications for the overseeing elders in the churches on the island of Crete, but did not mention deacons. A possible reason for this omission is that deacons were not yet needed because the churches were smaller and newly organized. Elders had to be established first before deacons were introduced. In a small congregation, the elders may be able to fulfill all of their shepherding responsibilities themselves without a need for deacons.

A Successful Deacons' Ministry

Good shepherds manage their resources effectively, always finding new ways to improve the health and growth of their flock. Likewise, conscientious shepherd elders are constantly looking for new, creative means of improving their work for the Lord and of mobilizing, organizing, and encouraging others in their work for the Lord.

Thus, a successful deacons' ministry is dependent largely on effective supervision by the elders. As many questions about deacons are not answered in Scripture, the elders have a great deal of flexibility in how to direct and utilize them. The elders need to use their God-given creative thinking powers and organizational skills to effectively utilize the ministry of the deacons. If not, the deacons will flounder and become frustrated with the elders.

ALL ARE "SERVANTS" OF THE CHURCH, SOME ARE "ASSISTANTS" OF THE ELDERS

Deacons work directly at helping the elders, relieving them of certain administrative and pastoral tasks. They are, as their title states, *assistants*. Because of their special position and work, they are required to meet specific, elder-like qualifications. In addition, they must be publicly examined by the church and its leaders as to their qualifications, and only if found above reproach, can they then serve as assistants to the elders. These qualifications are not required of all who serve in the church.

> *A successful deacons' ministry is dependent largely on effective supervision by the elders.*

There is a certain difference between assistants to the elders and other church leaders who serve the church body. Not everyone who leads a church ministry is an assistant of the elders. Nor should the whole church body be construed to be elders' assistants, although all members should work together under the elders' leadership in building up the church.

Regardless of which view of the role of deacons a congregation holds, a church *must make a distinction* between *all* who serve the church and *some* who serve in the church as official, qualified *diakonoi.* Furthermore, the pastor elders must determine precisely which tasks the deacons perform and which ones others in the congregation perform. If clear lines of responsibility are not delineated, there will be confusion and ineffective organization, which inevitably creates conflict among the members.

Every-Member Ministry

When considering the work of the deacons we must not forget that the entire congregation is to be a living, functioning body, with each member gifted by God and responsible for the life and work of the church. "The work of ministry" is the work of *all* the saints (Eph. 4:12). We cannot separate Paul's doctrine of elders and deacons from the doctrine of the Church as the living body of Christ. The Christian community is truly a "one-anothering community." In the body of Christ, *every individual member* of the body is responsible to work together with the other members to build up the body of Christ. Each member is responsible for loving, encouraging, exhorting, serving, admonishing, teaching, building up, caring for, praying for, and bearing the burdens of every other brother and sister in God's family.[10]

We cannot separate Paul's doctrine on elders and deacons from the doctrine of the Church as the living body of Christ.

This means that every member of the local church has a role to play if the church is to be a healthy, well-functioning body.[11] This doctrine is sometimes referred to as "every-member ministry of the body of Christ."[12] It is an exciting, relevant Christian doctrine that we must always keep in mind when addressing Paul's concept of deacons/assistants. As one writer so aptly puts it, "The functioning of the body requires, and is *equally* dependent on, those who are not leaders."[13]

Every follower of Christ is a "servant" (*diakonos*) of Christ (John 12:26) and is "to serve one another" (1 Peter 4:10). Thus deacons do not do everything in the church. The elders and even deacons are to recruit and mobilize their fellow members in the body to help accomplish the many tasks required of a growing, healthy church body. As the Scripture says, the whole body, only "when each part is working properly, makes the body grow so that it builds itself up in love" (Eph. 4:16).[†]

Deacons' Work as a Deliberative Body and as Individuals

In order to deal with certain assignments such as distributing resources to the needy, the deacons can meet together as a deliberative body on their own or together with the elders. Collecting and distributing charitable gifts, for example, should always be managed by several approved officials in order to protect the church from misappropriation of funds or scandal.[14] Other assignments, like hospital visits, important phone calls, or event arrangements can be delegated to individual deacons, based on needs and circumstances. Again, there is a great deal of flexibility in how deacons assist the elders.

"The functioning of the body requires, and is equally dependent on, those who are not leaders."
— Andrew D. Clarke.

[†]For further information on the biblical doctrine of every-member ministry in the body of Christ, go to www.deaconbook.com.

CONFLICT BETWEEN ELDERS AND DEACONS

Elders and deacons work together closely and share overlapping responsibilities. So it is inevitable (and common) that some decisions and situations will lead to conflict between them. But Scripture gives us proven principles for achieving harmonious working relationships in difficult situations.[‡]

Elders Clothed with Humility and Diligent in Their Work

Our Lord modeled and taught a distinctive, new style of leadership that is radically different from the world's methods. The Christlike leadership style requires humility, servanthood, gentleness, and self-sacrificing love.[15] For this reason, shepherd elders are forbidden by Scripture to use their God-given authority to act as rulers over those placed in their pastoral charge ("not domineering over those in your charge," 1 Peter 5:3). Elders are not to be autocratic or Diotrephes-like leaders (3 John 9–10).

Our Lord modeled and taught a distinctive, new style of leadership that is radically different from the world's methods.

Furthermore, the qualifications for elders require that they have a "gentle" spirit, and not be "violent," "quarrelsome," or "arrogant or quick-tempered" (1 Tim. 3:3; Titus 1:7). Addressing both the elders and younger members of the congregation, Peter exhorts both groups to act with humility toward one another if they are to please God and work together in harmony:

[‡]For the biblical principles for dealing with conflict, read Alexander Strauch, *If You Bite and Devour One Another: Biblical Principles for Handing Conflict* (Littleton, CO: Lewis and Roth, 2011).

> Be subject to the elders. Clothe yourselves, *all of you*, with humility toward one another, for "God opposes the proud but gives grace to the humble." (1 Peter 5:5; italics added)

If a church has biblically qualified elders who clothe themselves in humility, there will be less conflict. And when conflict does arise (and it will), Christlike attitudes and behaviors will enable elders to handle disagreement constructively.

In addition, shepherd elders need to be diligent in their pastoral oversight. If they are lazy, ineffective, uncommunicative, forgetful, or disorganized, or appear to be off-loading their responsibilities onto others, they will frustrate all those who serve under their leadership. This will damage relationships and create resentment and conflict. Elders need to be examples of wise leadership, hard work,[16] and effective delegation. They need to be good shepherds of God's sheep, like the Lord Jesus.

Deacons Clothed with Humility and Diligent in Their Work

The deacons' status as assistants to the elders needs to be expressed in humble, loving service to others. They must demonstrate "the fruit of the Spirit" (Gal. 5:22–23) and Christlike attitudes (Phil. 2:3–5) if they are to enjoy harmonious relationships with the elders and others with whom they work. Because they represent the elders, exercise a measure of authority over the congregation, and hold official titles, they can be tempted by pride, thinking too highly of themselves (1 Peter 5:5).

It is especially important for deacons to guard against a critical spirit toward their leaders, and against assuming they have more authority than is theirs. The deacons are not an independent church board of directors, checking and balancing the eldership. Like everyone else in the church, the deacons must "obey" and "submit" to their leaders (Heb. 13:17); they must "esteem them very highly in love because of their work," and "be at peace" with the elders (1 Thess. 5:12–13).

Deacons also need to be diligent in their work and follow through with their responsibilities. If they discourage the very people they are supposed to help, relationships will be strained. But if they do their work well, they will be an enormous help to the elders and to the health of the local church body. In addition, deacons "who serve well . . . gain a good standing for themselves and also great confidence in the faith that is in Christ Jesus" (1 Tim. 3:13).

> *The deacons are not an independent church board of directors, checking and balancing the eldership.*

Since the deacons assist the elders in their work, they must possess certain character qualities that are similar to those of the elders. In the next four chapters, we will explore the biblical qualifications required of the deacons.

Key Points to Remember:

1. The appointment of the table-serving officials by the twelve apostles provided Paul and the first churches he established with an apostolic precedent for the need and creation of an official position of assistants to the elders in the church (Acts 6:1–7).

2. Although the practical care of the church's poor, sick, and needy would be a core responsibility of the deacons, there would be other demanding tasks requiring the special help of the elders' qualified assistants.

3. Having formal assistants to help the elders would provide better pastoral care for the congregation, protect the elders from overwork, and free them to concentrate more effectively on their ministries of prayer and preaching the Word of God (Acts 6:2, 4).

4. Many questions about deacons are not answered in Scripture. So the elders have a great deal of flexibility in their direction of the deacons. Shepherding elders need to be creative and skilled to be able to effectively make the most of the ministry of the deacons.

5. Elders and deacons who obey scriptural principles for handling conflict can work together in humble harmony.

---

[1]The fact that Stephen and Philip were gifted teachers does not change the fact that these men were chosen by the whole congregation and appointed by the twelve apostles for the specific duty of serving tables (Acts 6:3). The fact that the Seven were appointed to serve tables did not bar them from other ministries for which they may have been gifted, such as teaching the Word or defending the faith. But these gifts were not among the qualifications set forth by the Twelve.

If Stephen and Philip seem to us overqualified for serving tables, were not the twelve apostles themselves both servants of the Word and servants of tables? The congregation's choice and the apostles' commissioning of these gifted men demonstrate how important the task of administrating the church's benevolence ministry was in the thinking of the first Christians. The congregation chose its best to care for its least.

Because Stephen and Philip preached, performed miracles, baptized, and confronted adversaries of the faith, must it be concluded that these were duties assigned to the table-serving Seven or to the later deacons? Philip baptized new converts (Acts 8), but *not* in his role as one of the seven officials administering the church's charitable aid. This was part of his evangelism work, conducted after he left Jerusalem.

By virtue of their Spirit-given gifts, Stephen and Philip preached the Word and performed "great wonders and signs among the people" (Acts 6:8; 8:6–8). Stephen and Philip's roles as preachers, teachers, and miracle workers were *not* the result of congregational selection or apostolic appointment, but of the gifting and leading of the Holy Spirit. Stephen and Philip were both administrators of charity relief by choice of the congregation, and gifted teachers of the Word by choice of the Holy Spirit. They were gifted men who took on more than one set of responsibilities; they functioned in different capacities at the same time.

[2]Acts 6:1; 11:27–30; Rom. 15:25–27; 2 Cor. 8:1–5; 8:6–9:15; Gal. 2:10.

[3]Acts 15:2, 4, 6–29; 16:4; 21:17–25.

[4]Acts 20:27–31; 1 Tim. 3:2; 5:17–18; Titus 1:9.

[5]Post-apostolic writers like Irenaeus, Hippolytus, Cyprian, Jerome, and Augustine believed that the table-serving Seven of Acts 6 were the first deacons. Methodically tracing the historical development of the ancient deacon, James Monroe Barnett succinctly summarizes this point: "The poor and needy had always been the major concern of the Church and were the special responsibility of the deacons" (*The Diaconate: A Full and Equal Order* [Harrisburg, PA: Trinity, 1995], 65).

[6]Peter Lampe, *From Paul to Valentinus: Christians at Rome in the First Two Centuries* (Minneapolis, MN: Fortress, 2003), 127.

[7]The deacon is ordained "to the service of the bishop, to do what is ordered by him" (Geoffrey J. Cuming, *Hippolytus: A Text for Students* [Bramcote Notts, England: Grove Books, 1976], 13).

[8]*The Apostolic Tradition of Hippolytus* 24; *Shepherd of Hermas, Similitude* 9.26.2 [103.2]; *Didascalia Apostolorum* 16, 18; *The Vision of Paul* 36; *The Constitutions of the Holy Apostles* 3.1.17, 3.3.19.

[9]The deacons of the Roman Catholic Church "serve in a balanced and integrated threefold ministry of Word, Sacrament, and Charity" (William T. Ditewig, *101 Questions and Answers on Deacons* [Mahwah, NJ: Paulist Press, 2004], 22).

[10]Rom. 15:2, 14; 1 Cor. 12:25; Gal. 5:13; 6:2; Col. 3:16; 1 Thess. 4:18; 5:11; Heb. 3:13; 10:24–25; James 5:16; 1 Peter 4:10; 1 John 4:7.

[11]Rom. 12:4–8; 1 Cor. 12:1–30; 14:1–40; Eph. 4:7–16; 1 Peter 4:10–11.

[12]John Stott, *The Living Church: Convictions of a Lifelong Pastor* (Downers Grove, IL: IVP Books, 2007), 76.

[13]Andrew D. Clarke, *A Pauline Theology of Church Leadership* (New York: Bloomsbury, 2008), 136.

[14]2 Cor. 8:19–21.

[15]Matt. 20:25–28; 23:1–12; Mark 9:33–37; 10:42–45; Luke 22:24–27. See also John 13:13–17.

[16]Acts 20:18–23, 26–35; 1 Thess. 5:12; 1 Tim. 5:17.

Part Three

THE DEACONS' QUALIFICATIONS, EXAMINATION, AND REWARDS

Deacons likewise must be dignified, not double-tongued, not addicted to much wine, not greedy for dishonest gain. They must hold the mystery of the faith with a clear conscience. And let them also be tested first; then let them serve as deacons if they prove themselves blameless. Their wives likewise must be dignified, not slanderers, but sober-minded, faithful in all things. Let deacons each be the husband of one wife, managing their children and their own households well. For those who serve well as deacons gain a good standing for themselves and also great confidence in the faith that is in Christ Jesus.

1 Timothy 3:8–13

Chapter 5

THE DEACONS' QUALIFICATIONS
1 TIMOTHY 3:8–9

In a letter to a young elder named Nepotian, Jerome, father of the Latin translation of the Bible, rebuked the churches of his day (AD 394) for showing more interest in the appearance of their church buildings than in the proper selection of their church leaders:

> Many build churches nowadays; their walls and pillars of glowing marble, their ceilings glittering with gold, their altars studded with jewels. Yet to the choice of Christ's ministers no heed is paid.[1]

It is sad to say, but the same careless attitude toward the biblical qualifications for elders and deacons exists in churches today. Yet Scripture makes the uncontested point that God's paramount concern is not with buildings or programs but with the moral and spiritual character of those who lead his people. For this reason, the church offices of elder and deacon are to be filled only by those who qualify according to God's standards as revealed in Scripture.

DEACONS "MUST BE"

In his first letter to Timothy, Paul lists the required standards for the deacons. Using the language of necessity to introduce the first five qualifications (vv. 8–9), Paul begins, "Deacons likewise must be . . ."

The adverb "likewise" (v. 8) means "similarly" or "in the same way." It introduces a new and distinct group of people, the *diakonoi*, that Paul compares with the previous group, the *episkopoi*.

To better understand the grammatical structure of this passage, we need to note that the words "must be" in verse 8 do not appear in the Greek text of verse 8, but need to be supplied from verse 2 of the Greek text:

Verse 2: Therefore an overseer must be (*dei . . . einai*) above reproach. (*Dei* is the verb of necessity; *einai* is the infinitive, "to be").

Verse 8: Deacons likewise [must be] dignified. "Must be" (*dei . . . einai*) is supplied from verse 2.

The point of the passage is straightforward: just as the overseers "must be" of a certain character in order to qualify for "the office of overseer" (1 Tim. 3:1–7), deacons also "must be" of a certain character to qualify for their position and work (1 Tim. 3:8–13). The qualifications are no less necessary for a deacon than for an elder.

Paul then lists the qualifications that a deacon must meet:

- Dignified (worthy of respect)
- Not double-tongued
- Not addicted to much wine
- Not greedy for dishonest gain
- Holding the mystery of the faith with a clear conscience

The Public Witness of the Gospel

Underlying the qualifications for elders and deacons is Paul's fierce concern for the public testimony of the local church and the truths of the gospel before an unbelieving, watching world.[2] He knew that the devil would use any failing on the part of the church's leaders to shame the church's public image (see verses 6–7). So, to protect the credibility of the gospel and the reputation of the local church from public ridicule, Paul insisted that the church's elders and deacons "be above reproach," morally and spiritually.

Thus the qualifications Paul lists are meant to safeguard the local church from unfit elders and deacons who could potentially disgrace the believing community. The qualifications are also intended to secure leaders who are qualified and equipped to lead and care for God's church. We now will examine the first five biblical requirements for deacons. The deacons addressed in verses 8–9 are male deacons. Women are not mentioned until verse 11.

To protect the credibility of the gospel and the reputation of the local church from public ridicule, Paul insisted that the church's elders and deacons "be above reproach," morally and spiritually.

"DIGNIFIED"

In the Lord's work, a leader's moral character and public reputation are essential to the task of leading God's people. That is why all elders must be "above reproach" in character and public reputation (1 Tim. 3:2; Titus 1:6). It then follows that those who officially assist the elders are to be of similar character and reputation, or as Paul writes, "dignified."

Today the word "dignified" might convey the idea of a person who is reserved and proper in appearance and demeanor. But that is not the best meaning of the Greek term (*semnos*) that Paul uses here. The term, *semnos,* is not easily translated into English. It describes a person whose attitudes and conduct win the admiration of others. It refers to a respectable, well-thought-of person. The New International Version better renders the term as "worthy of respect."[3]

A good example of a man who was "worthy of respect" was Timothy. Luke wrote that: "He was well spoken of by the brothers" (Acts 16:2). Timothy's character had earned him a good reputation, which is most commendable in a young man. This attribute qualified Timothy to travel with Paul and assist him with his gospel mission.

In the Lord's work, a leader's moral character and public reputation are essential to the task of leading God's people.

As highly visible officials in the church, deacons are expected to be role models of Christian character and living. Candidates for this office must demonstrate a respectable lifestyle, so that, upon public examination by the church and its leaders, they are found to be "blameless" in character (1 Tim. 3:10). "They must be," writes one commentator, "of good character and that certified by the public *testimony*."[4]

When the twelve apostles spelled out requirements for the selection of the table-serving Seven of Acts 6, they required that those selected be "of good repute" (Acts 6:3). "Of good repute" describes a person known and well-regarded by the congregation, a person who can be trusted to care for dependent widows and properly manage charitable donations. Like the twelve apostles, Paul was concerned about the public reputation of those who hold office in the church. As those who assist and represent the elders in their work, the deacons must be "worthy of respect."

Immediately following this requirement of public respectability, Paul points out three common vices: untruthful speech, abuse of alcohol, and financial greed. These sinful behaviors are particularly troublesome because of their potential to create disrespect among both Christians and non-Christians. Think of the politicians and religious figures, for example, who have been caught in lies, are known for habits of excessive drinking, or have embezzled public or charitable funds. These corrupt leaders have brought reproach upon their offices, and lost their reputations and the public's respect. When church leaders lie, embezzle, or are addicted to alcohol or other substances, they bring public reproach upon the Lord Jesus Christ and his Church. They have forgotten God's all-important call to his people to be holy as he is holy:

> *"You shall be holy, for I am holy." (1 Peter 1:16)*

> As obedient children, do not be conformed to the passions of your former ignorance, but as he who called you is holy, you also be holy in all your conduct, since it is written, "You shall be holy, for I am holy." (1 Peter 1:14–16)

"NOT DOUBLE-TONGUED"

The first of several prohibitions Paul stipulates is that a deacon not be "double-tongued." The word "double-tongued" or "double-worded" (*dilogos*) expresses the idea of saying one thing to one person and saying something different to another. So this qualification emphasizes integrity of speech and specifically prohibits any kind of "insincere"[5] or duplicitous speech.

Duplicity of speech ruins trust and undermines a leader's credibility. In contrast, truthful speech is the foundation of trust and promotes good working relationships among colleagues. Although this prohibition may seem like a minor issue, less-than-honest speech is damaging to relationships. It is like dead flies in precious ointment:

> Dead flies make the perfumer's ointment give off a stench;
> so a little folly outweighs wisdom and honor. (Eccl. 10:1)

Possibly this first prohibition is necessary because deacons are often placed between the elders and the people they are helping on behalf of the elders. When people are under pressure, it may be tempting to reveal less than the full truth, or to conceal the truth when speaking to certain people, or to think that "little white lies" are acceptable. And when there is disagreement or conflict, some people may try to please both parties by saying one thing to the elders and another thing to the people being helped. Inevitably, those who play loose with the truth, color the truth, or try to please everyone will be guilty of being "double-tongued." Such a person does not command respect and is a sad testimony to "the word of truth, the gospel of your salvation" (Eph. 1:13).

Truthful speech is the foundation of trust and promotes good working relationships among colleagues.

When a prominent Christian pastor was charged by the government with financial fraud and put on trial, for example, a newspaper quoted the prosecuting attorney's comment about the pastor: "He is a slippery talker; we may never be able to convict him." A "slippery-talking" pastor—indeed, any church leader—is an appalling witness to the gospel and the God of all truth: "Lying lips are an abomination to the Lord" (Prov. 12:22). Behind a deceitful tongue is a deceitful mind.

Scripture charges all believers, in all cultures and at all times, to renounce falsehood. We must speak truthfully to one another because we are all "members one of another" in the body of Christ:

> Therefore, having put away falsehood, let each one of you speak
> the truth with his neighbor, for we are members one of another.
> (Eph. 4:25)

In some societies speaking the truth to one another may not be culturally valued. Saving face is more important, even if one has to lie. But in the body of Christ, putting "away falsehood" and speaking "the truth" honestly to one another is the Christian standard of speech, even if it is uncomfortable and countercultural.

As church officials and examples of Christlike character, deacons must be known for integrity of speech. Our words have serious consequences, and Jesus warned that "every careless word [we] speak" will someday be judged by God (Matt. 12:36–37). So Jesus holds us responsible for what we say, as well as what we do. If a deacon's words cannot be trusted, he is not worthy of respect and is not fit to assist the elders in the care for God's church.

"NOT ADDICTED TO MUCH WINE"

It is unacceptable for the elders and deacons of God's household to be "addicted to much wine." This second prohibition is not an absolute ban on drinking, but a prohibition against excessive use of wine (and we might add, any other substance) that would damage any aspect of a person's reputation or service for God. This prohibition is in keeping with the Bible's many warnings against the potential dangers of wine and strong drink.[6] For example:

> Wine is a mocker, strong drink a brawler, and whoever is led astray by it is not wise. (Prov. 20:1)

> Who has woe? Who has sorrow? Who has strife? Who has complaining? Who has wounds without cause? Who has redness of eyes? Those who tarry long over wine. (Prov. 23:29–30)

In Titus 2:3, Paul forbids older Christian women from becoming "slaves to much wine." He expresses the same idea here in relationship to deacons. They are not to be enslaved to wine. "For whatever overcomes a person, to that he is enslaved" (2 Peter 2:19).

Enslavement to alcohol reveals a lack of Spirit-controlled living. A Christian with a drinking problem is controlled by the flesh, not by the Holy Spirit (Gal. 5:16–24), and as such is an appalling example of what a believer in Christ is to be like. Any addiction impairs one's judgment and connection to reality. Enslavement to alcohol may also lead to the sins of hypocrisy, uncontrolled anger, lying, or spousal abuse.

Furthermore, alcohol abuse interferes with a believer's growth in Christlikeness and with the work of the Holy Spirit in a believer's life. This is why Scripture says:

> And do not get drunk with wine, for that is debauchery, but be filled with the Spirit. (Eph. 5:18)

Of particular concern to church leaders should be the "secret alcoholic" (also called a "closet alcoholic" or "a high-functioning alcoholic"). Do not expect to see a deacon who is an alcoholic lying drunk in the street. It is more likely that he will be a secret alcoholic who leads a double life. He will be a master of concealment. He may work hard all day and appear to be responsible, even successful, but be inebriated at home during the evening hours. He will stubbornly deny his addiction and go to great lengths to hide it. He may aggressively attack anyone who exposes his problem, including his spouse and children. "Care-fronting" a functional alcoholic is a difficult and unpleasant experience because he is prepared to fight and lie to protect his addiction.

The secret alcoholic damages family relationships and will bring reproach upon the church and the office of deacon. People will ask, "How can that man have a drinking problem and still be allowed to be a deacon? Why don't the elders deal with this?" In God's holy family, a person enslaved to alcohol is not "worthy of respect" and is not qualified for church office.

"Not Greedy for Dishonest Gain"

The Bible repeatedly warns against the sin of greed and "the love of money . . . a root of all kinds of evils" (1 Tim. 6:10). It also presents many examples of leaders who used their God-given positions and authority to *acquire* financial gain at others' expense.[7] Luke, for example, exposes the heart condition of many of the religious officials our Lord encountered, accusing them of being "lovers of money" (Luke 16:14). Jesus accused the Pharisees of stealing from "widows' houses" (Luke 20:47). And the prophet Jeremiah bemoaned the fact that:

> From the least to the greatest of them, everyone is greedy for unjust gain; and from prophet to priest, everyone deals falsely. (Jer. 6:13)

"The love of money . . . [is] a root of all kinds of evils." (1 Tim. 6:10)

Thankfully, Scripture also includes examples of honorable leaders who did not use their official position, title, or influence to fleece the faithful of material assets. In his farewell message to the nation of Israel, the godly priest and judge, Samuel, testified that he did not abuse his position in order to steal from the people:

> "I have walked before you from my youth until this day. Here I am; testify against me before the Lord and before his anointed. Whose ox have I taken? Or whose donkey have I taken? Or whom have I defrauded? Whom have I oppressed? Or from whose hand have I taken a bribe to blind my eyes with it? Testify against

me and I will restore it to you." They said, "You have not defrauded us or oppressed us or taken anything from any man's hand." (1 Sam. 12:2–4)

A Prohibition for Leaders

No one was more sensitive to possible accusations of greedy motives and personal profiteering from the gospel than the apostle Paul. In his letters to Timothy and Titus, Paul warned about false teachers and their love of money that was evident in their materialistic motives.[8] God does not want his servants to be greedy-minded pilferers. God's standard is that the church's elders and deacons be concerned with giving, rather than getting, money. As Paul reminded the Ephesian elders:

> I coveted no one's silver or gold or apparel. You yourselves know that these hands ministered to my necessities and to those who were with me. In all things I have shown you that by working hard in this way we must help the weak and remember the words of the Lord Jesus, how he himself said, "It is more blessed to give than to receive." (Acts 20:33–35; see also Phil. 4:17)

As assistants to the elders, deacons often have access to church donations, and therefore cannot be "greedy for dishonest gain." The Greek term used here (*aischrokerdēs*) is a strong word emphasizing shameful, base, or fraudulent gain.[9] For example, in the disbursement of charitable funds during the New Testament period, most giving was cash or material goods. A greedy leader could easily skim off money for his own profit. Today a deacon could use his titled position and the people's trust to gain access to people's homes, bank accounts, inheritances, or insurance policies to enrich himself. So, for the protection of the church and its people, a deacon cannot be "greedy for dishonest gain."

A Powerful Temptation

For some, money can be a more powerful temptation than sex or alcohol. So we cannot be naïve about the temptations church leaders face. Stealing church donations or misappropriating church funds is a widespread problem. Even among the twelve apostles there was a thief. Judas acted as if he cared about the poor, but the apostle John explains his true motive:

> He said this, not because he cared about the poor, but because he was a thief, and having charge of the moneybag he used to help himself to what was put into it. (John 12:6)

Today, we hear too often of high-profile church officials caught embezzling church money. In certain parts of the world, the financial exploitation of God's people by church leaders is pervasive.[10]

No one was more sensitive to possible accusations of greedy motives and personal profiteering from the gospel than the apostle Paul.

In most cases, however, church officials do not steal actual cash. Instead, they misdirect church funds to their own so-called "ministry expenses": meals, travel, vacations, sports activities, and car and home repairs. Unless agreed upon by the congregation and its leaders, all such misappropriation of church funds is shameful profit. It is a betrayal of trust. It is fleecing the flock, not serving the flock.

People who do these kinds of shady financial dealings are often devoid of a pure conscience; they are self-deceived and full of self-justification. They resist having their financial decisions and practices questioned by others. They steal without remorse. They are morally corrupt.

Having a plurality of deacons and elders helps to provide built-in accountability in the administration of church finances. Believers are not usually going to give to the church if they do not trust the integrity of their leaders. In order to provide genuine accountability and transparency there must always be more than one person collecting and distributing church funds.

For this reason, when Paul was collecting and delivering the offerings from the Gentile churches for the poor believers in Jerusalem, he emphatically made the point that he (and others with him) carried and administered the offering in a way "honorable" before both God and people. Paul did not collect and deliver the offering alone:

> We take this course so that no one should blame us about this generous gift that is being administered by us, for we aim at what is honorable *not only in the Lord's sight but also in the sight of man.* (2 Cor. 8:20–21; italics added)

"Holding the Mystery of the Faith with a Clear Conscience"

A deacon must know the beliefs of the Christian faith, possess the faith, hold firmly to the faith, and live life consistently with "the mystery of the faith." Philip Towner nicely summarizes this fifth qualification for deacons:

> The qualification stipulates that the candidate's adherence to the faith ("holding to it") is to be unquestioned, and his conduct is to be appropriate to the faith he professes.[11]

The expression, "the mystery of the faith," is a Pauline phrase encompassing the distinctive truths of the gospel. In the New Testament, the term "mystery" (*mystērion*) most often means "revealed secret," a divine plan or purpose that was previously hidden and inaccessible, but then is revealed by God and proclaimed to all who will believe (see especially Rom. 16:25–26).

God chose Paul to be his special instrument for revealing his previously hidden plans, and Paul labored diligently to help all believers know "God's mystery, which is Christ, in whom are hidden all the treasures of wisdom and knowledge" (Col. 2:2–3).

"The Mystery of the Faith"

What, then, is the special nuance of the phrase, "the mystery of the faith"? The answer is found in the object of the mystery, "the faith," which here refers to the entire fixed body of Christian beliefs.[12] Today we find those beliefs in the New Testament. In Ephesus, the false teachers had distorted the faith, so it was imperative that those in official positions of authority in the church hold steadfastly to "the faith" as Paul proclaimed it.

This qualification for deacons is similar to the requirement that elders are to "hold firm to the trustworthy word as taught" by the apostles (Titus 1:9). Deacons, as well as elders, must be true to the faith.

A deacon must know the beliefs of the Christian faith, possess the faith, hold firmly to the faith, and live life consistently with "the mystery of the faith."

Living "with a Clear Conscience"

A deacon must adhere to apostolic doctrine "with a clear conscience." God has given everyone a self-judging faculty, a conscience or inner voice that speaks to us of what we believe to be right or wrong. The conscience "is man's inner awareness of the moral quality of his own actions."[13] Because the conscience both judges and guides a believer, he is not to go against that voice.

Whenever we act in a way contrary to "the faith," and do not seek forgiveness and correction, we defile our consciences, and that is sin. Every time a Christian violates his or her conscience, he weakens its convicting power and makes sin and hypocrisy easier to commit. Every believer is to continually educate the conscience so that it agrees with the truths of God's Word and not the standards of secular society.

A person who holds to the faith with a clear conscience is one whose profession of faith is matched and demonstrated by conduct that is consistent with the faith. As one writer explains: "The Christian maintains a clear conscience by living in harmony with the truths unveiled in God's Word."[14]

The New Testament does not allow believers to separate life and doctrine. It requires consistency between belief and practice. However, some professing Christians claim to hold to orthodox doctrine but *exhibit* unorthodox thinking and behavior. Over time they harden their consciences so that they are no longer convicted of sin and rebellion.

For Christians, such a serious disconnect between what they believe and how they live is unacceptable. "The mystery of the faith" is not abstract philosophy disconnected from one's daily ethical behavior and attitudes. The "knowledge of the truth," Paul taught, "accords with godliness" (Titus 1:1). So a deacon cannot hold to "the faith with a clear conscience" and live in sexual immorality, steal money from the poor, be a drunkard, hate a brother, or mix false theology with the truths of the gospel. Orthodox doctrine must be matched by orthodox behavior. So to qualify for the office, a deacon candidate must hold steadfastly to "the faith" and live a lifestyle consistent with the doctrines of "the faith."

Whenever we act in a way contrary to "the faith," and do not seek forgiveness and correction, we defile our consciences, and that is sin.

Deacons Not Required To Teach

Some scholars claim that the qualification, "hold the mystery of the faith with a clear conscience," indicates that deacons are to teach.[15] But this is an improbable interpretation because Paul's instruction to Timothy does not include directions about *teaching* the mystery of the faith. Instead Paul insists that a deacon *uphold* the faith with a good conscience.

The fact that deacons do not have to be "able to teach" does not imply that they *cannot* teach. Teaching is simply not related to their office. A person who holds the office of deacon can certainly *participate* in other church ministries that are outside his specific responsibilities as a deacon. In a small church, both elders and deacons often have to take on many tasks that are not specifically related to the core responsibilities of their office. They may, as the saying goes, have to "wear several hats."

The Necessity of Examination

But how are we to know if a deacon candidate believes and behaves consistently with the faith and is worthy of respect, or if, in fact, he lacks integrity in his speech, or is a secret alcoholic, or a greedy pilferer? Answers to these questions are found by instituting and observing the next qualification:

> And let them also be tested first; then let them serve as deacons if they prove themselves blameless. (1 Tim. 3:10)

Key Points to Remember:

1. To protect the credibility of the gospel and the reputation of the local church from public ridicule, the church's elders and deacons "must be above reproach," morally and spiritually.

2. A deacon must be a person worthy of respect, one whose attitude and behavior have earned the respect of others.

3. A deacon must demonstrate integrity of speech and self-control in the use of alcohol.

4. A deacon must demonstrate financial integrity. We cannot be naïve about the financial temptations church leaders face. Stealing church donations or misappropriating church funds is a widespread problem.

5. A deacon must hold firmly to the divine truths of Christian doctrine and model the gospel by a lifestyle consistent with the beliefs of his Christian faith.

---

[1]Jerome, "Letters 52," in *The Nicene and Post-Nicene Fathers*, 6: 94.

[2]Phil. 2:15; Col. 4:5–6; 1 Thess. 4:10–12; 1 Tim. 3:7; 6:1; Titus 1:13; 2:5, 8, 10.

[3]"Worthy of Respect" (*semnos*): NIV, CSB; "worthy of respect/honor, noble, dignified, serious" (*BDAG*, 919). For other uses of the adjective *semnos*, see Phil. 4:8; 1 Tim. 3:8; Titus 2:2; for the noun form, *semnotēs*, see 1 Tim. 2:2; 3:4; Titus 2:7.

[4]Richard B. Rackham, *The Acts of the Apostles*, Westminster Commentaries (London: Methusen, 1901), 83.

[5]"Double-tongued" (*dilogos*): "sincere," NIV; "not hypocritical," CSB; "insincere" (*BDAG*, 250).

[6]Prov. 20:1; 21:17; 23:20–21, 29–35; 31:4–5; Eccl. 10:17; Isa. 5:11, 22–23; 28:7–8; Hos. 4:11; Rom. 13:13; 1 Cor. 5:11; 6:9–10; 1 Thess. 5:7–8.

[7]Num. 22–24; 1 Sam. 2:13–17; 8:3; 2 Kings 5:20–27; Neh. 6:10–14; Isa. 22:15–25;

56:9–11; Ezk. 22:25, 27; Mic. 3:11; Matt. 21:13; Luke 11:39; Acts 8:9–24.

[8] 1 Tim. 6:3, 5–10; Titus 1:10–11; see also 2 Peter 2:3, 14–16.

[9] "Greedy for dishonest gain" (*aischrokerdēs*): "shamelessly greedy for money, *avaricious, fond of dishonest gain*" (*BDAG*, 29).

[10] Sunday Bobai Agang, "Radical Islam Is Not the Nigerian Church's Greatest Threat," *Christianity Today* (May 2017), 55–57; *The Cape Town Commitment: A Confession of Faith and a Call to Action* (Bodmin, United Kingdom: The Lausanne Movement, 2011), 55–57, 60.

[11] Philip H. Towner, *The Letters to Timothy and Titus,* NICNT (Grand Rapids: Eerdmans, 2006), 264.

[12] "The faith" (*pistis*): 1 Tim. 1:19; 4:1, 6; 5:8; 6:10, 21; 2 Tim. 3:8.

[13] J. N. D. Kelly, *The Pastoral Epistles*, BNTC (London: Adam and Charles Black, 1963), 47.

[14] Lawrence O. Richards, *Expository Dictionary of Bible Words* (Grand Rapids: Zondervan, 1985), 187.

[15] I. H. Marshall, *The Pastoral Epistles*, ICC (Edinburgh: T&T Clark, 1999) 487–88. Towner, *The Letters to Timothy and Titus*, 262. Dieter Georgi, *The Opponents of Paul in Second Corinthians* (Philadelphia: Fortress, 1986), 29–32.

Chapter 6

EXAMINATION
1 TIMOTHY 3:10

At Valleyview Church the deacons are the church's business committee. Their primary duty is to make financial and facility decisions. Once a year the pastor invites all members to meet after a Sunday evening service to choose new deacons. As everyone gathers around a whiteboard, the chairman of the deacon board asks for nominations. Several names are suggested and written on the whiteboard. The members who attend (and only a few do) then vote for two new deacons to replace the two whose three-year terms have expired. After the votes are counted, the newly elected deacons are installed, and the pastor closes the meeting in prayer. The entire process takes less than an hour.

Except for that closing prayer, the pastor and members engaged in no prayer about the choices being made, no serious consideration of the biblical qualifications for deacons, and no conscientious effort to examine whether each candidate's moral character, family life, and lifestyle were consistent with the faith. Such thoughtless procedures display disregard for, or possible ignorance of, the clear instructions and authority of Scripture and seriously weaken our churches.

PROSPECTIVE DEACONS MUST BE EXAMINED

In the previous chapter, we explored 1 Timothy 3:8–9, where Paul spells out five qualifications for deacons:

- Dignified (worthy of respect)
- Not double-tongued
- Not addicted to much wine
- Not greedy for dishonest gain
- Holding the mystery of the faith with a clear conscience

Immediately following these qualifications, Paul establishes the requirement for examination:

> And let them also be tested first; then let them serve as deacons if they prove themselves blameless. (1 Tim. 3:10)

Without this requirement to examine whether or not a deacon candidate possesses the necessary scriptural qualities for office, the qualifications listed in verses 8–9 are just empty words on a piece of paper. So admission to the office of deacon must be preceded by examination and approval by the church and its leaders.

The assessment of a prospective deacon's qualifications must be taken as seriously as that of an elder's (1 Tim. 5:22–25).

Furthermore, the assessment of a prospective deacon's qualifications must be taken as seriously as that of an elder's (1 Tim. 5:22–25). The process of examining a deacon candidate will require time and effort, just as it does with an elder. The fact that the deacons' office requires elder-like qualifications and examination by others indicates that there is something significant about the deacons' work, which makes sense in light of their role as assistants to the elders.

"And . . . Also"

Verse 10 begins: "And let them [deacons] also be tested first." The two conjunctions "and" (*de*) and "also" (*kai*) connect the deacons' testing with the implied testing of the overseers.[1] Thus a deacon candidate, like an elder candidate, must be tested first before being admitted into the office of deacon. However, some commentators deny that "and . . . also" refers to the overseers/elders of verses 1–7. They contend that these conjunctions simply add necessary precautionary factors to the five qualities mentioned in verses 8–9.

Although I prefer the former interpretation, either view of the phrase "and let them also" plainly summons deacon candidates to be "tested first" before they take office. Since there are scriptural qualifications required of deacons, by necessity there must also be some process for evaluating a candidate for possession of these biblical qualities.

"Tested First"

The Greek verb translated "tested" (*dokimazō*) means "to make a critical examination of something, to determine genuineness, to put to the test, to examine."[2] In ancient Greek literature, *dokimazō* was sometimes used in reference to the examination of a person's credentials for public office.[3] Similarly, Paul uses the term here to indicate that a candidate for the office of deacon must be formally and publicly examined in order to determine whether the individual meets the requirements laid down in verses 8–9 and 12. Furthermore, the Greek verb "tested" is an imperative verb, so the testing of a candidate is not optional. Indeed, "The whole process of assessment under consideration is mandatory."[4]

"First . . . Then"

Be careful not to overlook the important sequential words, "first" and "then." A proper sequence for becoming a deacon must be followed, and the examination of the candidate must come "first." If the outcome of the deacon candidate's screening is positive, "then," and only then, is the candidate eligible to serve as an assistant to the elders.

"The whole process of assessment under consideration
is mandatory." — Philip Towner

"Proven Themselves Blameless"

The second main verb, *diakoneō*, translated as "let them serve," is the verb form of the Greek noun *diakonos,* which is used here in a technical sense, meaning to serve as deacons/assistants.[5] However, "let them serve" is conditional and the condition that must be met before serving as a deacon is summarized by the word "blameless": "Then let them serve as deacons if they prove themselves blameless."[6] In other words, the examination of the candidate's character and conduct according to the biblical requirements has shown nothing that would disqualify the person.

Being examined and shown to be "blameless" does not imply that the deacon is free of faults! All of us have character flaws, idiosyncrasies, and character traits that annoy others. Being proved "blameless" or "above reproach" relates specifically to the *qualifications* for office. A deacon who is found "blameless" in this regard is worthy of respect, truthful in speech, self-controlled in the use of wine, sound in doctrine and life, and a faithful husband, good father, and competent household manager. Of such people the psalmist says, "Blessed are those whose way is blameless" (Ps. 119:1).

If the outcome of the deacon candidate's screening is positive, "then," and only then, is the candidate eligible to serve as an assistant to the elders.

The Deacons' Significance

One might think that the qualifications for deacons require less enforcement than the qualifications for elders. But that is not so. Paul's rulings on the deacons' moral and spiritual qualities demonstrate that he considered them to be a significant body of officials in the church. He did not intend that the deacons' position and function be ignored or treated with contempt. It is just as important for deacons to be examined regarding their qualifications as it is for elders. This requirement demonstrates the significance of deacons to the church and its elders.

It is quite possible that the deacons in Ephesus were treated as irrelevant as a result of the false teachers, who proudly claimed special knowledge[7] and the prominent status of teachers. These pseudo-teachers would not have had much regard for the role of the deacons since they were not teachers, but viewed as underlings of the elders. But by placing the deacons alongside the overseers (vv. 1–7) and listing similar elder-like qualifications for the deacons (vv. 8–12), Paul corrects any such false notion of deacon irrelevance.

Because the deacons' role is so significant, an unfit deacon can cause many distressing problems in the church: hurt innocent people, disgrace the public reputation of the church, and be a burden to the elders, rather than a help.

These God-given qualifications for deacons protect the church from unfit and unworthy deacons. And, if necessary, these objective standards allow the church and its leaders to remove a sinful or dysfunctional deacon from office.

EXAMINING A DEACON FOR OFFICE

Paul does not provide a procedural manual for examining, approving, and installing a deacon candidate. Just as the New Testament is silent about specific procedures for administering the Lord's Supper and baptism, so too it does not give us detailed procedures for examining a deacon candidate. Paul simply states: "And let them also be [examined] first" (1 Tim. 3:10).

Unlike the book of Leviticus, the New Testament allows a great deal of freedom for conducting such matters. Detailed methods for selecting, examining, approving, and installing church officers are left in the hands of the local church and its leaders. The church's size and cultural context are factors in determining the specifics. A church of one thousand, for example, will have to do things differently than a church of fifty. Scripture only prescribes (1) the qualifications for deacons, (2) the necessity for examination by others, and (3) the warning to avoid hasty appointments to office (1 Tim. 3:8–12; 5:22).

Timothy to Oversee the Process of Examination

The verb for "examined" is an impersonal, passive, third-person plural.[8] So who is to conduct such an examination? In the case of the troubled church in Ephesus, Timothy, Paul's official (but temporary) delegate, most likely oversaw the process of examining and approving a deacon or elder for office. Both Timothy and Titus had received authority from Paul to make such decisions, to "command," to "teach," to "appoint," and to "rebuke with all authority" (1 Tim. 5:7; 6:2; Titus 1:5; 2:15; 3:8).[9]

But Timothy could not have properly evaluated a prospective deacon without the help and advice of those who knew the candidate. Furthermore, he would have needed to show due respect for the elders in the selection of their assistants.

Most likely, Timothy would have worked closely with the elders and congregation, assisting them in the examination process of a prospective deacon or elder. Timothy would have followed Paul's customary style of Christlike, servant leadership and not exerted his authority over the church in a heavy-handed manner.[10]

Scripture only prescribes (1) the qualifications for deacons, (2) the necessity for examination by others, and (3) the warning to avoid hasty appointments to office (1 Tim. 3:8–12; 5:22).

Elders to Oversee the Process of Examination

When the time came for Timothy (or his replacement) to leave the church at Ephesus, the elders would have taken the lead in appointing new deacons in conjunction with the congregation's participation. It would now be the elders' responsibility to initiate and supervise the important process of finding, training, examining, approving, and installing new deacons.

As congregational leaders, the elders oversee the process of decision-making and problem-solving by making recommendations and ensuring that what is done is done "in love" (1 Cor. 16:14), in an orderly manner (1 Cor. 14:40), and according to sound principles of group decision-making.[11] Moreover, they instruct the congregation in how to examine a candidate according to scriptural standards and, most important, protect the congregation from disruptive people and destructive internal conflict.

Public Examination

The examination and approval of elders and deacons is one of the most important decisions a congregation and its leaders make in the life of the church.[12] Examining a potential deacon's qualifications for office is part of the responsibility that comes with living together as members of the family of God. *Therefore, the congregation is not to be passive in the examination of its officers.*

As a tightly-knit family of brothers and sisters in Christ, every member needs to be involved in decisions that affect them all. The office of deacon, like the office of elder, is a public office in the church, and the qualifications for deacons are written in Scripture for the entire church family to know and enforce. So the examination of a prospective deacon is to be a public matter, not a private decision made by a few people.

In his letters to his churches—and this is a significant fact—Paul always addressed the entire congregation, which included its leaders (Phil. 1:1). He held the congregation and its leaders responsible for building up one another, maintaining unity, and for solving its own internal problems. Because of the close, reciprocal relationship between a congregation and its elders, the goal should always be to speak and act as a united family of brothers and sisters.[13]

One thing the New Testament is absolutely clear about—and there should be no debate about it—is this: Christlike love, humility, servanthood, gentleness, peaceableness, prayer, and faithfulness to the Word are to characterize all relationships, deliberations, and disagreements in the church, even during times of serious conflict and division of opinion.

Thus, God calls the congregation to "respect," "esteem very highly in love," "honor," "obey," and "submit to" its leaders (1 Thess. 5:12–13; 1 Tim. 5:17; Heb. 13:17) and warns the elders not to lord their authority "over those in [their] charge" (1 Peter 5:3). Biblically minded leaders should have—like all the biblical writers—a high view of God's people as the "new creation" in Christ (2 Cor. 5:17; Gal. 6:15). Those whom the elders lead are "saints," "priests," brothers and sisters in Christ, and fellow members of the living body of Christ. Biblical elders are not rulers over their subjects, nor priests over laity. Thus they sincerely desire to listen to, consult with, and seek the wisdom of their fellow members of the body of Christ and family of God.

This requires a great deal of free and open communication between the elders and the congregation, the leaders and those led. Good leadership always demands good communication with those who are being led. Tragically, too many church leaders are poor

> *Good leadership always demands good communication with those who are being led.*

communicators and the congregations too passive. This should not be!

Procedures and Objections

A variety of procedures can be used in examining a potential deacon's qualifications for office. Regardless of the procedures used, members of the congregation must be allowed the opportunity to freely express their questions, doubts, or approval of a candidate for the office of deacon. This may be done either verbally or in written form such as through a deacon evaluation survey. Since God's Word provides an objective, public standard, everyone is responsible to see that God's requirements for deacons are followed.

The elders need to investigate any objections or accusations voiced against a candidate's character in order to determine if the person making the objection is correct. If the objection or accusation proves to be unfounded, it should be dismissed. Since 1 Timothy 3:10 refers to the assessment of a candidate's character according to the requirements articulated in verses 8–12, members of the congregation must limit their objections to those that are scripturally based. For example, a biblical objection would be, "The candidate abuses alcohol," not, "I'm voting with my friends," or "I just don't like the person in question." God's written Word, not personal preferences or prejudices, must govern God's household and its leaders. As one biblical commentator puts it: "The basis for evaluation should be scriptural requirements, not a candidate's personality or social or professional status."[14]

The office of deacon, like the office of elder, is a public office in the church, and the qualifications for deacons are written in Scripture for the entire church family to know and enforce. So the examination of a prospective deacon is to be a public matter, not a private decision made by a few people.

No Hasty Appointments

No hasty or surprise appointments of new elders or deacons should be made. No one should be considered for the office of deacon who is not already serving as an active member of the church and who is not known by the congregation. Yet, we hear stories of pastors or deacon boards asking an individual who has attended the church for only a few weeks to become a deacon. Such unwise practices directly violate the Scripture's warning not to appoint or lay hands on a person too quickly:

> Do not be hasty in the laying on of hands . . . The sins of some people are conspicuous, going before them to judgment, but the sins of others appear later. So also good works are conspicuous, and even those that are not cannot remain hidden. (1 Tim. 5:22, 24–25)

Paul is referring here to the appointment of an elder to office, but the same principle applies equally to the office of deacon. No one should be appointed to office if the church has not first invested the time and effort to properly examine the candidate's character and credentials. Obviously, this cannot be accomplished unless the candidate has been serving in the church for some period of time and is known by the congregation and its leaders. A careful examination will reveal any disqualifying sin or hindrance, and will also bring to light the hidden strengths of a potential deacon.

Installing a Deacon into Office

After a prospective deacon has been approved for office, some form of public recognition is in order. The first Christians were not averse to simple, public ceremonies for appointing or commissioning fellow members to special positions or tasks.[15] The laying on of hands was used to publicly install the table-serving Seven into their new position (Acts 6:6).

In Paul and Timothy's day, public recognition of a new deacon was likely expressed by the laying on of hands. First Timothy 5:22 indicates that hands were placed on the elders at the time of their appointment to the eldership. The appointment of deacons may have followed the same practice.

The installation of a deacon before the congregation by the laying on of hands (or any other means the church desires to use) officially and publicly places the person into office. It says to the newly appointed deacon, "You now officially begin your responsibilities. You have the authority to do the work of a deacon. You can now use the title 'deacon.' You have important work to do." Installation of a deacon says to the congregation, "Here is a new deacon to assist your elders in the care of God's church. This person is biblically qualified and approved by the church and its leaders."

Think It Through; Make It Better

In all matters pertaining to the examination, approval, and installation of a church officer, we should follow the scriptural principle that "all things should be done decently and in order" (1 Cor. 14:40). Whatever procedures you use to select, examine, approve, and install a prospective deacon, think them through carefully. Continue to evaluate their effectiveness and improve the process. You can always make it better! Fight against the tendency to be thoughtless, lazy, or irresponsible in the examination and appointment of your elders or deacons.

Whatever procedures you use to select, examine, approve, and install a prospective deacon, think them through carefully. Continue to evaluate their effectiveness and improve the process. You can always make it better!

Key Points to Remember:

1. The process of examining a deacon candidate requires time and effort, just as it does with an elder.

2. The Greek verb translated "tested" (*dokimazō*) means "to make a critical examination of something, to determine genuineness, to put to the test, to examine."

3. It is the responsibility of the overseeing elders to initiate and supervise the important process of finding, training, examining, approving, and installing new deacons.

4. The examination of a prospective deacon is to be a public affair, not a private decision made by a few people. The congregation is not to be passive in the examination of its officers.

5. Continue to sharpen and improve your procedures for selecting, examining, training, approving, and installing new deacons.

---

[1]See 1 Timothy 5:24–25.

[2]*BDAG*, 255. Also "of the examination of prospects for special service in the Christian community . . . 1 Ti. 3:10" (*BDAG*, 255).

[3]See Ceslas Spicq, *TLNT* 1: 357; Walter Grundmann, "*dokimazo*," in *TDNT*, 2: 256; Hermann Cremer, "*dokimazō*," in *Biblico Theological Lexicon of New Testament Greek*, trans., W. Urwick, (1895; repr. Greenwood, SC: The Attic Press, Inc., 1977), 699–700.

[4]Philip H. Towner, *The Letters to Timothy and Titus*, NICNT (Grand Rapids: Eerdmans, 2006), 264.

[5]"Let them serve" (*diakoneitōsan* from *diakoneō*): "to carry out official duties, minister" (*BDAG*), 229.

[6]"Blameless" (*anegklētos*). This same word is used in Titus 1:6 of the elders. It is a synonym of "above reproach" (*anepilēmptos*) in 1 Timothy 3:2, referring to overseers. So both the elders and deacons must be blameless or above reproach.

[7]1 Tim. 1:3–7, 19–20; 4:1–3, 7; 6:3–5, 20–21.

[8]I. H. Marshall comments: "The impersonal passive form of the verb (*dokimazesthosan*) may suggest the whole community is in mind (Roloff, 164; Acts 6:3); but it is possible that leaders would bear the primary responsibility" (*The Pastoral Epistles*, ICC [Edinburgh: T&T Clark, 1999], 492).

[9]William D. Mounce's comment on Timothy and Titus' identity bears repeating:
Timothy and Titus stand outside the church structure. They are not bishops or elders and are not members of the local church. They are itinerant, apostolic delegates sent with Paul's authority to deal with local problems. . . . Timothy and Titus are never told to rely on their institutional position in the local church for authority; rather they rely on the authority of Paul and the gospel (*Pastoral Epistles*, WBC [Nashville, TN: Nelson, 2000], lxxxviii).

[10]1 Cor. 4:21; 2 Cor. 1:23–24; 6:3–10; 10:1, 8; 13:9–10; Phil. 1:25; 1 Thess. 2:5–12; 2 Tim. 2:24–26. For a biblical exposition of loving, servant leadership, see Alexander Strauch, *A Christian Leader's Guide to Leading with Love* (Littleton, CO: Lewis & Roth, 2006).

[11]Group decisions should be made based on explicit biblical principles; reasoned arguments; honest and open discussion; listening to all sides of an issue; weighing the pros and cons; being willing to change; seeking the corporate wisdom of God's people; being guided by facts and evidence; stopping misbehavior by an angry, out-

of-control member; and seeking the best decision. The body of elders is a microcosm of the larger church body, and thus the elders must use the same principles in making their decisions together. Finally, be aware of the inherent dangers and weaknesses of group decision-making.

12"These [newly appointed overseers], therefore, who were appointed by them [the original overseers] or, later on, by other reputable men *with the consent of the whole church*" (*1 Clement* 44:3; italics added); "Therefore *appoint for yourselves* bishops [overseers] and deacons worthy of the Lord" (*Didache*, 15.1; italics added); see also *The Epistles of Cyprian* in *The Ante-Nicene Fathers*, vol. 5 (5.4; 32.1; 64.3; 67.4, 5).

13Rom. 15:5–6; 1 Cor. 1:10; 2 Cor. 13:11; Phil. 1:27; 2:2–5; 4:2–3; 1 Peter 3:8–12.

14Andreas J. Köstenberger, "1–2 Timothy, Titus," in *Expositor's Bible Commentary*, vol. 12, rev. ed. (Grand Rapids: Zondervan, 2006), 529.

15Acts 6:6; 13:3; 1 Tim. 4:14; 5:22; 2 Tim. 1:6.

Chapter 7

WIVES
1 TIMOTHY 3:11

We have spelled out five qualifications for the office of deacon found in verses 8–9. Immediately following these verses is the all-important requirement that all deacon candidates be publicly examined as to their qualifications. Then, and a bit unexpectedly, a list of four qualifications for certain women appear: "[*Gynaikas*] likewise must be dignified, not slanderers, but sober-minded, faithful in all things" (v. 11). But who are these women (Greek, *gynaikas*): the wives of the deacons or certain women officeholders?

I must begin by stating that whether this passage addresses the wives of deacons or women deacons, Scripture instructs all Christian women to be actively engaged in "the work of ministry, for building up the body of Christ" (Eph. 4:12). Like Christian men, Christian women are priests, saints, and Spirit-gifted servants of Christ and his people. They play essential roles in the ministry of the local church and world evangelism.

So, even if 1 Timothy 3:11 addresses the deacons' wives only, women are still to be engaged in significant mercy ministries or other vibrant ministries within the church. A woman does not need to be a deacon to participate in mercy ministries or to be part of a committee organized to serve others.

This leads me to comment on a matter that is very important to me. Although this book asserts that deacons are the official assistants to the elders and that the women referred to in 1 Timothy 3:11 are the wives of the deacons, this does not lessen in the slightest way the contribution of multitudes of women deacons or deaconesses who have poured out their lives to serve in their local church. Even if the structure of a church is not exactly according to Scripture, the people who serve sacrificially as deacons or deaconesses are biblical servants of Christ and do a great service to the Lord's people. Like the Lord Jesus, they love his Church and have given themselves for her. To them the Scripture says:

> God is not unjust so as to overlook your work and the love that you have shown for his name in serving the saints, as you still do. (Heb. 6:10)

Scripture instructs all Christian women to be actively engaged in "the work of ministry, for building up the body of Christ" (Eph. 4:12).

WOMEN, WOMEN DEACONS, DEACONESSES, HELPERS, WIVES

One of the problems we immediately face when interpreting the meaning of 1 Timothy 3:11 has to do with the Greek word *gynē* (pronounced, goo-NAY). In the Greek language, *gynē* is the standard word for an adult woman or wife. Only the context determines whether *gynē* should be translated as "woman" or "wife."

Furthermore, Paul provides no qualifying word, modifying phrase, or definite article to identify clearly the women to whom he refers. Thus the translator or commentator must add a word or phrase to help clarify for the English reader who these *gynaikes* are (*gynaikes* is the plural form, meaning women/wives; pronounced goo-NAI-kes). In addition, translators usually include a footnote in order to acknowledge the alternative interpretations of *gynaikas*.

The *English Standard Version*, for example, adds the possessive pronoun "their," making the women of verse 11 the wives of deacons. It also adds the footnote: "Or Wives, likewise, must, or Women, likewise, must." The *New International Version* renders the phrase, "In the same way, the women are to be worthy of respect" adding the footnote, "Possibly deacons' wives or women who are deacons."

Gynē/Gynaikes

Gynē = woman/wife (pronounced, goo-NAY)

Gynaikes = women/wives (the nominative plural, pronounced goo-NAI-kes)

Gynaikas = women/wives in verse 11 is the accusative plural of *gynē* (pronounced goo-NAI-kas)

As a result of the ambiguity of the original language used, there are five views on the identity of the women of 1 Timothy 3:11.

1. All Christian women in general: This view claims that although Paul is listing the qualifications for male deacons, he interjects into the middle of the passage four character qualities necessary for all the "women" of the church: "dignified, not slanderers, but sober-minded, faithful in all things." The advocates of this view claim that it was not uncommon for Paul to interject extraneous ideas into his flow of thought (e.g., 1 Tim. 5:22–25).

2. Women deacons: The proponents of this view are very clear about what they mean. They emphatically insist that, just as there are male deacons, 1 Timothy 3:11 introduces women deacons. These women are fully equal with the men deacons, and all serve together in the same office. Thus, these women should be called deacons, not deaconesses or women helpers. The *Revised English Bible* translates verse 11 as "women in this office," clearly stating that the women are fully deacons.

3. Deaconesses: A third view argues that the women addressed in verse 11 form a third group of officials in the church that is distinguished from but similar to the male deacons. Thus there are elders, deacons, and deaconesses. Proponents of this view often use "deaconesses" and "women deacons" interchangeably, and many use the term "women deacons" but mean "deaconesses," *a separate group who are not full-fledged deacons.* There are different variations of this view (often not clearly articulated), but generally those who hold this view believe deacons are men and deaconesses are women. Deaconesses primarily serve the women of the church.

4. Women helpers or assistants to the deacons: The proponents of this view deny that the women of 1 Timothy 3:11 are deacons or deaconesses. Instead, they claim that the women addressed are a separate order of women who minister to other women and to the poor and needy of the church. These women assist the deacons, but they have no official title. They are referred to as "women helpers," "assistants," or "ministering women."

5. The deacons' wives: This view understands that when listing the requirements for deacons, Paul adds that the deacons' wives also must have appropriate qualifications. Like their husbands, they must be of a certain character: "dignified, not slanderers, but sober-minded, faithful in all things."

The *English Standard Version*, as well as other versions, adds the possessive pronoun "their" to *gynaikas* in verse 11: "*Their* wives likewise must be dignified." The possessive pronoun "their" is not in the original Greek text. It is added by the translators who interpret these *gynaikes* to be the wives of the deacons. Many, if not most, English Bibles translate *gynaikas* as wives.[1]

Although sound Bible teachers can be found who advocate almost any one of the above views, my conclusion is that Paul is referring to the deacons' wives (see View 5). In order to avoid getting bogged down with weighty, technical arguments for these different views, in the Appendix I will present the basic evidence that the *gynaikes* of verse 11 are the wives of deacons. For a thorough examination of the arguments for and against the other views, go to www.deaconbook.com.

QUALIFICATIONS

For the sake of brevity and consistency, I will refer to the following four qualifications in light of the view of this book, that the women of verse 11 are the wives of deacons. However, these same qualifications apply to any of the other views. If the women of verse 11 are deacons, deaconesses, or women helpers, these qualifications are appropriate for their entrance into office or service.

Dignified

The first quality, "dignified," is identical to the deacon's requirement in 1 Timothy 3:8. Just as a deacon must be "dignified" (or "worthy of respect"), his wife must be "dignified." In the Lord's work, a leader's moral character and public reputation are critical to his task of leading God's household. The qualification "dignified" describes a person whose attitudes and conduct win the respect of others.

So, a deacon's wife must be a respectable, well-thought-of person. Furthermore, she must have "a good name" (Ecc. 7:1), which a person earns by being godly in character and lifestyle. Obviously, a godly wife will greatly enhance her husband's reputation as a deacon. She will be one of the most important influences on his development of Christlike character and his work in the church. As the Scripture says,

> An excellent wife is the crown of her husband, but she who brings shame is like rottenness in his bones. (Prov. 12:4)

> A prudent wife is from the Lord. (Prov. 19:14)

> An excellent wife who can find? She is far more precious than jewels. . . . She does him good, and not harm, all the days of her life. (Prov. 31:10, 12)

A godly wife will greatly enhance her husband's reputation as a deacon. She will be one of the most important influences on his development of Christlike character and his work in the church.

Not a Slanderer

Our God is the God of truth and justice, but a slanderer is not concerned about truth and justice, only with striking back, tearing down, finding fault, or venting anger. So it should not surprise us that the Old Testament laws for holy living prohibited slander and hate:

> You shall be holy, for I the LORD your God am holy. . . . You shall not go around as a slanderer among your people and you shall not stand up against the life of your neighbor: I am the LORD. You shall not hate your brother in your heart, but you shall reason frankly with your neighbor, lest you incur sin because

of him. You shall not take vengeance or bear a grudge against the sons of your own people, but you shall love your neighbor as yourself: I am the LORD. (Lev. 19:2, 16–18)

The Greek word for "slanderers" (*diabolous*), used here as an adjective, is the same Greek word for *devil* (*diabolos*).[2] Like the devil, whom Jesus declared to be "the father of lies" (John 8:44), a slanderer spreads lies, false rumors, malicious gossip, and innuendos, and is capable of inflicting long-term, irreparable damage on relationships and the reputations of others. These days, by means of social networks, blogs, chat rooms, or even email, slanderers are able to cause even more damage than ever before. The anonymity of the Internet provides increased incentives for any accuser or faultfinder seeking to inflict harm.

Slanderers, or "malicious talkers" (NIV), are often controlled by anger, jealousy, bitterness, or wounded feelings, and they may even believe the lies and accusations they are spreading. To be sure, slanderers will deny that they are slanderers or gossips. They will justify their malicious behavior by claiming to have spiritual discernment, "a word from God," or even be "speaking the truth in love." Such persons may even think they have the "gift of criticism," even though there is no such gift. No wonder Solomon wrote: "Whoever utters slander is a fool" (Prov. 10:18).

Clearly a believer cannot command respect if he or she has a reputation for spreading gossip or making false accusations. The local church cannot be a holy community if hate and slander are not stopped and publicly judged as sin (1 Cor. 5:11–13).

A deacon's wife will have access to confidential information about people and their needs that others in the congregation will not have. If she is a slanderer or "malicious talker" and uses sensitive information to gossip and cause conflict, she will be a serious detriment to the elders and deacons, as well as to the whole church. In many cases, the targets of her slander will inevitably be the elders and deacons themselves (see 1 Tim. 5:19), therefore undermining the entire leadership of the church. So, just as a deacon must demonstrate integrity of speech, his wife must demonstrate integrity of speech. She cannot be the kind of woman who freely speaks evil of others.

A believer cannot command respect if he or she has a reputation for spreading gossip or making false accusations.

Sober-minded

There are very few secrets in a local church environment. People know the wives of the deacons and elders and know the influence—good or bad—that they have on their husbands and the church. So a deacon's wife must be "worthy of respect," free from a negative reputation for slander, and known to be "sober-minded," demonstrating stable behavior and balanced judgment.

The Greek word for "sober-minded" (*nēphalios*) can mean sobriety in the use of wine, that is "temperate," or it can be used figuratively for sobriety in mind, conduct, and judgment. If the term is used figuratively in verse 11 (which is here preferred),[3] it describes a woman who is stable, self-controlled, level-headed, and free from debilitating excesses. Of course, any excessive use of wine would be included in this qualification. Some commentators think that both the ideas of balanced mental judgment and excessive use of wine are included in the term.

A deacon's wife must be level-headed and balanced because of her strong influence on her husband. Furthermore, because husbands and wives often talk about such matters together, a deacon's wife will sometimes know sensitive information about people in the church and their problems. If a deacon's wife lacks self-control and balanced mental judgment, she may adversely influence her husband's judgment and work. She will probably undermine his reputation in the congregation too.

A deacon's wife must be "worthy of respect," free from a negative reputation for slander, and known to be "stable-minded," demonstrating stable behavior and balanced judgment.

Faithful in All Things

Paul's final and comprehensive qualification for the deacon's wife is not charm or skilled work, but "faithful in all things." The word "faithful" here means "dependable," "reliable," or "trustworthy." The deacon's wife is to be a completely trustworthy person.

We might expect Paul to say that deacons' wives must be faithful to God or to their families. Instead, he writes, "faithful in all things." That means they are to be faithful ("trustworthy" or "reliable") in every sphere of life: in their commitment to Christ and his Word, in their duty to family, in their witness to neighbors, in all relationships, and in all responsibilities to the church family. Every aspect of the life of a deacon's wife is to be marked by faithfulness, dependability, and reliability, so that she is worthy of respect and is a blessing to the whole church.

In the end, a person's strong faith in Christ and the gospel is what produces a life of faithfulness in all things. When Paul wrote the letter of 1 Timothy, some women in the church had "already strayed after Satan" (1 Tim. 5:15). They were unfaithful to their professed commitment to Christ, the gospel, and their brothers and sisters. So Paul emphasized that a deacon's wife must be dependable, reliable, and trustworthy in all of her commitments.

Every aspect of the life of a deacon's wife is to be marked by faithfulness, dependability, and reliability, so that she is worthy of respect and is a blessing to the whole church.

The scriptural requirements for deacons, including their wives, provides more evidence of Paul's high esteem for the office of deacon. Paul intends that the role of deacons, as subordinate assistants of the elders, should not be minimized or overlooked by the church body, by the elders, or even by the deacons themselves. Let us not underestimate the significance of deacons to the local church, or misrepresent the biblical position and role of the deacons.

Key Points to Remember:

1. A deacon's wife must be worthy of respect. She is to be the kind of woman whose demeanor and conduct cause others to think well of her.

2. A deacon's wife must not be a slanderer. She cannot spread gossip, make false accusations, put people down, or constantly find fault, especially since she is privy to sensitive information.

3. A deacon's wife must be sober-minded and self-controlled. She should have balanced judgment, display stable behavior, and be free from debilitating excesses.

4. A deacon's wife must be faithful, reliable, dependable, and trustworthy in character and in all her commitments to God, family, and church.

---

[1]"Wives": KJV, NKJV, NIV (1984), ESV, CSB, Goodspeed, Phillips, MNT, Godbey, NET Bible, GNT, NLT, NEB.

[2]See 1 Tim. 3:6–7; 2 Tim. 2:26.

[3]If the four qualifications for deacons' wives in 1 Timothy 3:11 are meant to parallel the five qualifications for male deacons in verses 8–9, then we should translate the Greek term for "sober-minded" as "temperate," as in sobriety in the use of alcohol. However, in 1 Timothy 3:2, *nēphalios* is a positive quality required of the overseer. It is best translated there as "sober-minded" because of what follows in verse 3: an overseer is not to be "a drunkard." Surely Paul is not warning elders twice about the use of alcohol.

Also, both the verb and adjective forms of *nēphalios* are consistently used in the New Testament in the figurative sense of sobriety in one's thinking or lifestyle. See the verb form *nēphō* in 1 Thess. 5:6, 8; 2 Tim. 4:5; also 1 Peter 1:13; 4:7; 5:8 (*eknēpsate*, sober up; come to your senses). In Titus 2:2 *nēphalios* is used of older men; here the same problem exists of how to translate the term (see *New International Dictionary of New Testament Theology and Exegesis*, 2nd ed. [Grand Rapids: Zondervan, 2014], 3: 390–91).

Chapter 8

Marriage, Children, and Household
1 Timothy 3:12

For the first Christian churches, marital and family issues were critically important to their spiritual well-being and survival. Family issues were also essential to the believers' witness in an unfriendly society that was already suspicious of the people called "Christians." Thus, Christians who had stable marriages and households helped to deflect criticism by showing that Christians were a benefit, not a threat, to society. Moreover, having well-ordered families made the message of the gospel far more appealing to unbelievers.

All of these factors required that the leaders of the local churches have exemplary households. So Paul insisted that elders and deacons be above reproach in their marital and family lives:

> Let deacons each be the husband of one wife, managing their children and their own households well. (1 Tim. 3:12)

"The Husband of One Wife"

Like the elders, deacons must be "the husband of one wife." This phrase, and its related phrase "the wife of one husband" occur four times in the New Testament and only in the letters of 1 Timothy and Titus. Referring to the overseer in 1 Timothy 3:2, Paul insists

that,"an overseer must be above reproach, the husband of one wife."
In Titus 1:5–6, Paul uses the same phrase for the overseeing elder:

> Appoint elders in every town as I directed you—if anyone is
> above reproach, the husband of one wife.

Again, for the deacon in 1 Timothy 3:12, Paul writes:

> Let deacons each be the husband of one wife [*miâs gynaikos andres*].

For the dependent widow in 1 Timothy 5:9, Paul uses the feminine
version:

> Let a widow be enrolled if she is not less than sixty years of age,
> having been the wife of one husband [*henos andros gynē*].

The phrase "the husband of one wife" is made up of three Greek
words (*miâs gynaikos andres*; 1 Tim. 3:12). Because this three-word
phrase is ambiguous and appears only in the verses above, there
is disagreement over its meaning. Some commentators interpret the
phrase "the husband of one wife" to mean that a deacon can have
only one wife in a lifetime, even after the death of a spouse. Others
hold that the phrase prohibits a polygamist from church office.
Another interpretation excludes a once divorced and remarried
man from being an elder or deacon. Still others believe the phrase
requires a deacon or elder to be married.

In order to deal thoroughly with these different interpretations,
I have placed on my website (www.deaconbook.com) an in-depth
assessment of these various views of the phrase "the husband
of one wife."

This rare and unusual phrase is puzzling and difficult to interpret
with confidence. But by eliminating the views that conflict with the
overall biblical teaching on marriage (e.g., views like no remarriage

for a deacon after the death of his spouse) and by interpreting the phrase as a positive marital quality within the qualification lists for church officeholders and dependant widows, we can arrive at a reasonable solution.

Marital Faithfulness

"The husband of one wife" qualification is most likely a Pauline idiom emphasizing the positive virtue of fidelity in marriage, with marriage defined by Paul and Jesus as the "one flesh" union of one man and one woman (Matt. 19:4–6; Eph. 5:31–32).

The phrase addresses the candidate's character and reputation as applied to his wife, or even to other women. The phrase encapsulates "the characteristic of being devoted exclusively to one's spouse."[1] It is "a moral quality which is currently being demonstrated."[2] A few scholars answer the question, "What kind of man is the candidate for office?" with the paraphrase, "He is a one-woman type of man."[3] The emphasis is on the leader's character as demonstrated in being faithful and true to his wife.

The phrase ["the husband of one wife"] encapsulates "the characteristic of being devoted exclusively to one's spouse."

An elder or deacon candidate may be technically married to only one woman, but have the reputation of being a womanizer and, therefore, not be qualified as "the husband of one wife." Any man involved in marital infidelity, cohabitation, womanizing, or an unscriptural divorce and remarriage is disqualifed from church office.

Why, we might ask, did Paul not directly say "a faithful husband," or spell out clearly *not* an adulterer, a polygamist, or the divorced and remarried? This question can be asked of any of the various interpretations of the phrase "the husband of one wife." Whatever his reasons, it is certain that Paul was acutely aware of how fundamentally important it was to the spiritual health of the local church and its witness that its leaders' relationships with their spouses be "above reproach," neither dubious nor scandalous.

It must not go unsaid that this three-word phrase by itself cannot answer the many complex questions often raised about divorce and remarriage in the case of elders and deacons. Many painful and controversial questions are not answered by the requirement "the husband of one wife." Such issues need to be handled from the perspective of the whole of the Scriptures' teaching on marriage, divorce and remarriage, forgiveness, grace, and restoration—as well as its instructions on leadership example, the full spectrum of qualifications for elders and deacons, and their moral and spiritual fitness for office.

Whether or not agreement is reached on the precise meaning of the phrase "the husband of one wife," an elder or deacon must be above reproach in his marriage relationship as defined by the teachings of the whole of Scripture on sexuality and marriage.

An elder or deacon must be above reproach in his marriage relationship as defined by the teachings of the whole of Scripture on sexuality and marriage.

God Designed Marriage

Marriage as God intended is breathtakingly beautiful in its design. From the first three chapters of Genesis, and from our Lord's own teaching, we know that marriage was divinely instituted by a good God for the blessing and pleasure of humanity. God created the human race male and female and designed marriage to be a unique, one-flesh relationship of the two. From the beginning, the Creator intended marriage to be:

- A "one flesh" relationship between one man and one woman, a monogamous, heterosexual union (Gen. 2:18–25; Matt. 19:4–6)
- A sacred, covenant relationship witnessed by God himself (Mal. 2:13–16; Matt. 19:6)
- A permanent union (Matt. 19:6; Rom. 7:2)
- A sexual union for the procreation of the human race and intimate pleasure of the man and woman in a loving relationship (1 Cor. 7:2–5)
- An exclusive relationship in which "no other human relationship must interfere"[4] (1 Thess. 4:2–8; Heb. 13:4)
- A relationship symbolic of Christ and his Church (Eph. 5:25–32)

In his book, *God, Marriage, and Family: Rebuilding the Biblical Foundation*, Andreas J. Köstenberger defines biblical marriage in this way:

> The biblical concept of marriage is best described as a covenant, *a sacred bond between a man and a woman, instituted by and publicly entered into before God (whether or not this is acknowledged by the married couple), normally consummated by sexual intercourse.*[5]

Problems of Marital Infidelity and Perverse Practices

But when sin entered the world (Gen. 3), marriage became one of the first casualties. The war of the sexes began (Gen. 3:16), as did marital infidelity and every kind of perverse sexual practice imaginable, including incest (see Lev. 18). In fact, a key strategy in Satan's never-ending war on God's people is the destruction of the marriages of their leaders.[6]

In the Greco-Roman society in which the gospel of Christ first spread, marital infidelity was rampant and adversely affected the first Christians. Thus the New Testment writers repeatedly warned believers not to conform to the world's perverse sexual practices and marital infidelities.[7] To the Christians at Ephesus, Paul gives this ominous warning:

> But sexual immorality and all impurity or covetousness must not even be named among you, as is proper among saints. Let there be no filthiness nor foolish talk nor crude joking, which are out of place . . . For you may be sure of this, that everyone who is sexually immoral or impure, or who is covetous (that is, an idolater), has no inheritance in the kingdom of Christ and God. (Eph. 5:3–5)

A key strategy in Satan's never-ending war on God's people is the destruction of the marriages of their leaders.

God's people are to be living examples of God's design for marital oneness and sexual purity. Biblical prohibitions against any violation of our holy God's sexual and marital standards are meant to protect his people from the terrible human misery that sexual and marital sin produces. Moreover, God-honoring marriages enhance the mental, emotional, and spiritual health of children and help to protect children from the many dangers of this world.

For these reasons, the state of the elders' and deacons' marriages and families is of utmost importance to God and to the well-being of the local church. In order to protect the church, God has established specific marital requirements for its elders and deacons.

Therefore, the local church must insist that its leaders meet the "husband of one wife" requirement before and during their time in office. If this requirement is not enforced by the congregation and its leaders, the local church will begin a steady slide toward unbiblical marital and sexual practices.

Biblical prohibitions against any violation of our holy God's sexual and marital standards are meant to protect his people from the misery that sexual and marital sin produces.

"Managing Their Children and Their Own Households"

The final requirement for the deacon stipulates that he be able to capably manage his children and household. The spiritual quality of individual households in the local church significantly affects the spiritual quality of the larger household of God, the local church. If the individual households of the elders and deacons are dysfunctional, the larger church will also be dysfunctional and will project a pathetic witness to society.

A Father Who Manages His Children Well

The Christian father must not be passive, disinterested in his children, or neglectful of their needs: "A child left to himself brings shame to his mother" (Prov. 29:15). He should provide for his children financially, emotionally, physically, and spiritually. He must care about and contribute to their education and spiritual development. Above all, the Christian father must invest in healthy relationships with his children.

Elton Trueblood puts the seriousness of this qualification into proper perspective:

> No matter how much a man may be concerned with his work in the world, he cannot normally care about it as much as he cares for his family. This is because we have, in the life of the family, a bigger stake than most of us can ever have in our employment. We can change business associates . . . we can leave a poor job . . . but we cannot change *sons*. If we lose the struggle in our occupational interests, we can try again, but if we lose with our children our loss is terribly and frighteningly *final*.[8]

In this sinful world, there are no perfect, problem-free children or parents. We are all flawed sinners who constantly need godly guidance and help. Since "folly is bound up in the heart of a child" (Prov. 22:15), even the best fathers and mothers face problems and struggles with their children. So the requirement that the deacon be a father who manages his children "well" is not a demand for perfection. Rather, it describes a father who is actively engaged in the process of wisely and properly guiding his children through life's many struggles, failures, and problems, some of which can be severe.

The Leadership, Teaching, and Discipline of Children

In the context of fatherly responsibilities and household supervision, the term "managing" combines the ideas of leading and caring for.[9] Paul is referring to household leadership by a Christian father, not the kind of leadership customary in the military, business, or government. Specifically, this responsibility is the fatherly role of "managing," "leading," or "caring for" one's children in a capable, godly way. The emphasis in the text is on the adverb "well," which can also be translated "competently" or "proficiently."

A father who manages his children "well" . . . is actively engaged in the process of wisely and properly guiding his children through life's many struggles, failures, and problems.

In God's wise design for the family, the father plays a central role in the encouragement, instruction, and discipline of his children:

And these words that I command you today shall be on your heart. You shall teach them diligently to your children, and shall talk of them when you sit in your house, and when you walk by the way, and when you lie down, and when you rise. (Deut. 6:6–7)

Fathers, do not provoke your children to anger, but bring them up in the discipline and instruction of the Lord. (Eph. 6:4)

Fathers, do not provoke your children, lest they become discouraged. (Col. 3:21)

For you know how, like a father with his children, we exhorted each one of you and encouraged you and charged you to walk in a manner worthy of God, who calls you into his own kingdom and glory. (1 Thess. 2:11–12)

Besides this, we have had earthly fathers who disciplined us and we respected them. (Heb. 12:9)

Children need constant teaching, guidance, protection, discipline, and lots of love and affirmation. A Christian father is to be a teaching father who seizes every opportunity to instruct his children in the gospel and the Christian way of life. He is to live the Christian faith before his children and not be a religious hypocrite. He is to help his children grow up loving and revering the Lord. If he is diligent, his children will benefit greatly and so will he: "A wise son makes a glad father" (Prov. 10:1).

Furthermore, a Christian father should be a disciplinarian, but he may not use his fatherly authority in ways that provoke his children to unnecessary anger and frustration. In disciplining his child, the Spirit-guided father must always display "the fruit of the Spirit," not "the works of the flesh" (Gal. 5:19–23). In short, he is to be a Christlike father.

A Christian father is to be a teaching father who seizes every opportunity to instruct his children in the gospel and the Christian way of life.

He must not be a spirit-crushing father who gains submission through harsh discipline or unreasonable household rules. In some cases, such fathers have driven their children to abandon the faith.

Meeting the Biblical Requirement

The home is the first and best testing ground of a man's abilities to manage people and problems in a godly way. How can deacons help the elders in caring for other people with problems if they cannot deal with their own families' issues? Therefore, when assessing a prospective candidate's ability to do the work of a deacon, a key factor is how he manages his children. So the examination process (1 Tim. 3:10) must include a careful assessment of the candidate's parental and supervisory abilities.

But judging a man's competence as a father can be a tricky business, and may even be divisive to the church. People have different ideas of what a competent father looks like, and some situations are not clear-cut. Moreover, people have different philosophies of child rearing. All fathers have their weaknesses and faults. So to answer some of these complex and agonizing questions, the overarching qualifications in verses 1 Timothy 3:2, 8, "above reproach" and "dignified" (or "worthy of respect") must guide the church and its leaders in making a right assessment of a man's competence as a father.

The Management of His Household

A deacon must be a godly model of the Christian husband, father, and household manager who is known for his proven competence in managing his entire household. These domestic requirements do not dictate that he be married or have a family of a certain size or social standing. Paul simply deals with the usual situation that the prospective deacon has a wife, children, and a household. He insists that a deacon be above reproach in his marital relationship, fatherly leadership of his children, and supervision of his household, proving that he is able to assist the elders with the care of the congregation.

We must not overlook the fact that a household in the ancient world often included not only one's wife and children—the nuclear family—but also relatives such as a widowed mother or elderly father, household servants, and often those involved in the family business. A deacon candidate needs to show good management of those who live or work under his leadership. He is to maintain harmony in the home. His household must be stable and not be on the verge of collapse because of mismanagement.

The candidate's household must not be like the selfish households described in 1 Timothy 5:3–16 that had abandoned the care of their own poor widowed relatives. Instead of "learn[ing] to show godliness to their own household[s]" (v. 4), they expected the church to provide for their widows. Paul was unsparing in his disgust and condemnation of their greed and selfishness:

> But if anyone does not provide for his relatives, and especially for members of his household, he has denied the faith and is worse than an unbeliever. (1 Tim. 5:8)

Although wealth and prominent social status led to public office in Greco-Roman culture, the biblical qualifications for elders and deacons do not bend to the world's values. So there is no requirement that a deacon be rich, own a home, or have a large household. But if he does, he must be able to manage his children and household properly.

Just because a believing man has social status and material success does not automatically suggest that he be a candidate for the office of elder or deacon. No matter how gifted, successful, rich, knowledgeable, or charismatic a man may be, if he is not "the husband of one wife," does not manage his children according to God's principles, or cannot supervise his household properly, he does not qualify to be a deacon. These biblical qualifications for deacons help to protect the Lord's community from the rich and influential who might think they automatically deserve recognition in the church because of their achievements elsewhere.

Just because a believing man has social status and material success does not automatically suggest that he be a candidate for the office of elder or deacon.

Key Points to Remember:

1. Marital and family issues are critical to the spiritual health of the local church and its witness in an unfriendly society suspicious of the people called "Christians."

2. The phrase "the husband of one wife" is a distinctive Pauline expression for marital faithfulness.

3. God has established a firm marital standard for his church's elders and deacons. If it is not enforced by the church and its leaders, both will quickly sink into secular society's marital chaos and sexual immorality.

4. Capable management of any children a prospective deacon may have is a prerequisite for the office of deacon.

5. Capable management of one's household demonstrates a potential deacon's readiness for his responsibilities as assistant to the elders.

---

[1]Sidney Page, "Marital Expectations of Church Leaders in the Pastoral Letters," *Journal for the Study of the New Testament* 50 (1993), 113–14.

[2]Page, "Marital Expectations of Church Leaders in the Pastoral Letters," 113–14.

[3]Ed Glasscock, "'The Husband of One Wife' Requirement in 1 Timothy 3:2," *Bibliotheca Sacra* 140 (July–Sept. 1983), 250–52. Also William D. Mounce, *Pastoral Epistles*, WBC (Nashville, TN: Thomas Nelson, 2000), 170–73.

[4]Andreas J. Köstenberger, *God, Marriage, and Family: Rebuilding the Biblical Foundation*, 2nd ed. (Wheaton, IL: Crossway, 2010), 78.

[5]Köstenberger, *God, Marriage, and Family*, 78.

[6]For example, in the Old Testament, when the small group of Israelites came back to Jerusalem from their seventy-year exile, some of them intermarried with pagan idol worshippers. Even worse, Israel's leaders led in this violation of God's prohibition against intermarriage with idolaters: "In this faithlessness the hand of the officials and chief men has been foremost" (Ezra 9:2). Ezra, the reformer and biblical scholar, responded to this outright disobedience of God's marital laws with one of the greatest prayers of the Bible, a confession of sin and repentance, and a plea for God's forgiveness:

As soon as I heard this, I tore my garment . . . and sat appalled. Then all who trembled at the words of the God of Israel, because of the faithlessness of the returned exiles, gathered around me while I sat appalled . . . And at the evening sacrifice I rose from my fasting, with my garments and my cloak torn, and fell upon my knees and spread out my hands to the LORD my God, saying: "O my God, I am ashamed and blush to lift my face to you, my God, for our iniquities have risen higher than our heads, and our guilt has mounted up to the heavens. . . . Seeing that you, our God, have punished us less than our iniquities deserved and have given us such a remnant as this, shall we break your commandments and intermarry with the peoples who practice these abominations? . . . Behold, we are before you in our guilt, for none can stand before you because of this." (Ezra 9:3–6, 13–15)

7Rom. 13:13; 1 Cor. 5; 6:9–11; 7:1–5; 10:8–9; 2 Cor. 12:21; Gal. 5:19; Eph. 5:3–7; Col. 3:5; 1 Thess. 4:3–7; Heb. 12:15–16; 13:4; 1 Peter 2:11; 4:3–5; 2 Peter 2:14; Rev. 2:14, 20–21; 9:21; 21:8; 22:15.

8Elton Trueblood, *Your Other Vocation* (New York: Harper and Row, 1952), 82.

9William D. Mounce points out that,

This double nuance of leadership and caring is visible when Paul asks how someone who cannot manage his own household can be expected *epimeleisthai*, "to care for," God's household (1 Tim. 3:5). Leaders are not to be autocrats; they are servant leaders, following the model of Christ as a leader (*ho hēgoumenos*) who serves (*ho diakonōn*); Luke 22:26 (*Pastoral Epistles*, WBC [Nashville, TN: Thomas Nelson, 2000], 178).

Chapter 9

REWARDS
1 TIMOTHY 3:13

Paul was a master teacher and motivator. Because the heretical teachers at Ephesus caused such terrible conflicts within the church, Paul knew that the elders and deacons needed a positive word of encouragement. So he begins 1 Timothy 3 by assuring the present elders and potential new ones that the work of pastoral oversight is a necessary, valuable, and praiseworthy work. He affirms the honorable nature of the office and work of the church overseers with a "trustworthy" saying:

> The saying is trustworthy: If anyone aspires to the office of overseer, he desires a noble task. (1 Tim. 3:1)

Paul does the same for the deacons. In 1 Timothy 3:13, he concludes his list of deacon qualifications with the assurance that those who serve well as assistants will be (1) highly esteemed by the church body and (2) gain greater confidence in their personal faith relationship with Christ:

> For those who serve well as deacons gain a good standing for themselves and also great confidence in the faith that is in Christ Jesus. (1 Tim. 3:13)

Any idea that deacons are insignificant, or that their qualifications are not as necessary as those required of the elders, is hereby dispelled. Positive rewards await the deacons who perform their duties well. All deacons need to know these God-given, encouraging promises of rewards.

COMMENDABLE SERVICE

The text before us specifically addresses "those who serve well as deacons." Here, the term "serve"[1] is used in the technical sense, referring to one who serves in an assistant role. The adverb "well," which modifies "serve," indicates commendable performance in serving as an assistant. It is not "perfunctory office bearing"[2] that is commendable, but diligent service that is rewarded. Thus those "who serve well as deacons"—not necessarily all who are deacons—acquire "a good standing for themselves."

Deacons who serve diligently "gain," or acquire, certain benefits. These benefits are not received the moment they assume office but through the course of assisting the elders and serving the Lord's people. Deacons who "serve well" are conscientious, responsible, hard-working, sacrificial, and effective in their duties. They take initiative, follow through on their duties, and are serious and proficient in their work. Through such faithful service, a deacon acquires an honorable reputation and a deeper, more confident faith in Christ. As biblical commentator William Mounce so aptly explains:

> It is not so much that by being a good deacon a person will receive rewards; it is in the actual doing of the service that one daily acquires a better standing before the people and more confidence in one's personal faith. These rewards are not given to a believer at a certain time, but rather, are achieved during the process of service.[3]

It is not "perfunctory office bearing" that is commendable, but diligent service that is rewarded.

An Honorable Standing

The first promised reward is a "good standing." But what is this "good standing" the diligent deacon may gain for himself? The Greek word for "standing" (*bathmos*) literally means "a step" in a staircase or "a base of a pedestal." Some scholars take *bathmos* to mean that the deacon who serves well will be promoted to the next step in the church hierarchy, that is, to "the office of overseer." But this interpretation is highly unlikely. Even if a person is an outstanding deacon for many years and does his work exceptionally well, he is not automatically promoted to the office of overseer. In order to be an overseeing elder, a person must be able to teach and be called by the Holy Spirit to such an office (Acts 20:28). So it is possible that a deacon, even an exemplary one, may never qualify for "the office of overseer."

Paul's whole purpose in verse 13 is to encourage the deacons in their work and "to enhance the value of the office, just as at 3:1 he enhanced the office of [overseer]."[4] He is not seeking to push deacons from one office to another.

The "standing" Paul refers to has to do with reputation, and it is "a good standing," or, better yet, "an excellent" or "honorable standing." So it is more likely that Paul is teaching that the hard-working deacon will acquire a good reputation, not a "better" step up (or standing) in the hierarchy of church leadership.

To gain "a good standing" is to be held in high regard by the believing community and to be recognized and appreciated by the church family. Most likely "a good standing" will result in greater influence and moral authority in the church. What a privilege and blessing to enjoy an honorable standing among God's people!

GREAT CONFIDENCE IN THEIR FAITH IN CHRIST

The first benefit of assisting well focuses on the deacon's public reputation before people, but the second reward is far more remarkable. The first reward was people-focused—a good standing in the eyes of the congregation. The second reward is Christ-focused—a deeper personal faith in Christ and a closer relationship with Christ Jesus.

Paul promises that those who serve well as deacons will gain "great confidence in the faith that is in Christ Jesus." It is an intriguing fact that the challenging work of assisting the elders with the care of God's church significantly enhances their faith relationship with Christ. What a powerful encouragement this reward provides for all present and potential deacons!

To gain "a good standing" is to be held in high regard by the believing community and to be recognized and appreciated by the church family.

"Great Confidence"

The word "confidence" translates a significant New Testament Greek term, the noun *parrēsia* (meaning "boldness," "confidence," "assurance," "courage," "openness," "frank speech").[5] In the context of 1 Timothy 3:13, the noun *parrēsia* can be translated "boldness" (NRSV, CSB, KJV), "confidence" (ESV, NASB), "assurance" (NIV), or to "speak boldly" (TEV, NEB). The various English translations of *parrēsia* demonstrate that it is difficult to find agreement on what is the precise nuance of the term in this context. My preference is to translate the term as "confidence," while understanding that the ideas of assurance and boldness shade into the Greek word for confidence.

The confidence that deacons acquire for themselves is "great" confidence, which implies a considerable or significant degree of confidence. All deacons already possess faith in Christ because they are believers in Christ, and, to qualify as deacons, they have to "hold the mystery of the faith with a clear conscience" (1 Tim. 3:9). But the reward for diligent service is a *significant* increase in one's confidence in one's faith in Christ. The diligent deacon's faith in Christ is enlarged, deepened, strengthened, and emboldened.

> *The second reward is Christ-focused—a deeper personal faith in Christ and a closer relationship with Christ Jesus.*

"In the Faith That Is in Christ Jesus"

Whatever the precise translation of *parrēsia* is, this "great confidence" concerns the deacon's personal faith in Christ. The two prepositional phrases ("in faith," and "in Christ Jesus") specify the sphere (or realm) in which this "great confidence" is active. This confidence is not in a church leader or in one's abilities or knowledge. It is not arrogance, presumption, or brash self-confidence. Rather, it is greater confidence in one's faith in Christ.

In this passage, the noun "faith" is not used in the sense of a fixed set of Christian doctrines or the content of what one believes (see 1 Tim. 3:9). Instead, "faith" refers to one's personal faith, belief, or trust in Christ.[6] It is the deacon's own personal daily trust and belief in Christ.

In the Christian life, faith is the central, fundamental means of maintaining our ongoing relationship with Christ and God.

By faith our relationship with Christ is sustained, deepened, and strengthened. By faith we walk with Christ and draw near to him in a closer relationship. So Paul's assurance that deacons gain "great confidence in the faith that is in Christ Jesus" (1 Tim. 3:13) is directed to the deacon's personal faith "in Christ Jesus." Paul commonly uses this double designation, "Christ Jesus": "Christ" refers to his title (Messiah, God's Anointed One), and "Jesus" to his personal earthly name. So the deacon's faith is emphatically a Christ-focused faith.

A believer cannot put trust in anyone greater than the incomparable God-man, Christ Jesus. We can put our total and complete trust in him because he is completely trustworthy. His Word is truth and his promises are sure. Jesus never fails! What a wonderful thing it is to gain great confidence in one's faith in Christ Jesus.

The Christian life begins with faith in Christ for salvation. The Christian life also is lived moment-by-moment through active, ongoing faith in Christ, which includes trusting his teachings and promises as found in Scripture. In the process of serving well as assistants to the elders and ministering to the church family, deacons will gain a deeper and enlarged faith in Christ. They will see their personal relationship with Christ—which is by faith—strengthened, encouraged, and sustained.

In the Christian life, faith is the central, fundamental means of maintaining our ongoing relationship with Christ and God. By faith our relationship with Christ is sustained, deepened and strengthened. By faith we walk with Christ and draw near to him.

Deacons who have gained a deeper confidence in their faith in Christ are stronger, more mature, stable Christians. They have a greater love for Christ, greater understanding of God's Word, greater love for his people, greater commitment to Christ and the church, and make greater personal sacrifices of their time and money. Could deacons gain anything better than great confidence in their personal faith relationship with Christ, growing deeper and closer to their Savior and Lord?

What a wonderful conclusion these words are to the biblical instructions on deacons. How encouraging Paul's statements would have been to the first deacons of the church in Ephesus, and so they should be for the deacons in every church and in every generation.

Deacons Do Significant and Needed Work

That the deacons are a significant and needed help to the local church and its leadership should now be clear by the evidence presented throughout this book, based on a careful exposition of 1 Timothy 3:8–13. We have tried to be good Berean Bible students and examine the Scriptures thoroughly. As a result of our study we have observed that:

(1) Deacons are always linked to the overseers/elders, and like the elders, deacons hold an officially recognized office/position in the local church (Phil. 1:1; 1 Tim. 3:8–13).

(2) Deacons are subordinate to the overseers, as the terms *episkopos* and *diakonos* themselves indicate.

(3) Deacons must meet certain biblical qualifications that are similar to the qualifications for the overseers/elders (1 Tim. 3:8–10, 12).

(4) Deacons, like the elders, must be publicly examined as to their qualifications and fitness for office (1 Tim. 3:10).

(5) Unlike the elders, deacons are not required to be able to teach sound doctrine and refute false teachers (Titus 1:9).

(6) Deacons are not given a specific list of responsibilities. The elders determine the deacons' responsibilities.

(7) Deacons can gain notable respect from the congregation and see their faith relationship with Christ greatly enhanced and deepened as a result of their diligent service.

(8) Deacons, as the Greek word *diakonoi* best indicates within the context of 1 Timothy 3, are assistants.

These observations lead to the conclusion that deacons are the formal assistants to the pastor elders. Deacons best assist the elders by helping them keep their focus on their own supremely important tasks of feeding, leading, and protecting God's flock by God's Word, the Scriptures. Certainly, having qualified helpers enables the elders to provide God's church with better pastoral care, protects the elders from unhealthy overwork, and frees them to concentrate more effectively on prayer and "the ministry of the word" (Acts 6:4).

Like the early Berean Christians, you will now need to examine the biblical evidence and arguments of this book and decide for yourself "if these things [are] so" (Acts 17:11). May this book help restore the deacons to their original apostolic purpose and role in the local church.

Key Points to Remember:

1. Deacons who serve well will be held in high regard by the church family.

2. Deacons who serve well will gain a deeper faith and stronger relationship with Christ Jesus their Lord.

3. Deacons who have gained great confidence in their faith in Christ are stronger, more mature, stable Christians.

---

[1] "Serve," *diakonēsantes*, the participial form of the verb *diakoneō*.

[2] George W. Knight, III, *The Pastoral Epistles: A Commentary on the Greek*, NIGTC (Grand Rapids: Eerdmans, 1992), 173.

[3] William D. Mounce, *Pastoral Epistles*, WBC (Nashville, TN: Thomas Nelson, 2000), 205.

[4] B. B. Warfield, "Some Exegetical Notes on 1 Timothy," *Presbyterian Review* 8 (1887), 506.

[5] Paul uses the noun *parrēsia* eight times with the following possible meanings: 2 Cor. 3:12 (great openness); 7:4 (much confidence); Eph. 3:12 (boldness); Eph. 6:19 (boldness); Phil. 1:20 (all openness or boldness); Col. 2:15 (openness); 1 Tim. 3:13 (great confidence); Philem. 8 (boldness). See Acts 2:29; 4:13, 29, 31; 28:31 for boldness or openness to proclaim the message of salvation. Paul uses the verb form *parrēsiazomai* in Eph. 6:20 (speaking boldly, freely, openly), and in 1 Thess. 2:2 (having courage); see also Acts 9:27, 28; 13:46; 14:3; 18:26; 19:8; 26:26.

[6] This type of personal, subjective faith is mentioned in 1 Tim. 1:5, 14, 19; 2:15; 6:12; 2 Tim. 3:15.

Appendix

THE DEACONS' WIVES

If you have not read Chapter 7, "Wives," you will need to read it before reading this Appendix. Chapter 7 lists the various views that have been offered in identifying the women of verse 11:

- All Christian women in general
- Women deacons (coequals with male deacons)
- Deaconesses (a third, separate office)
- Women helpers, or assistants to the deacons
- Deacons' wives

For a thorough examination of the arguments for and against each of these views, go to www.deaconbook.com.

Although the wives-of-the-deacons view has fallen out of favor with most biblical commentators today, I propose that it remains a strong, defensible position and should not be brushed aside as an outdated interpretation. Proponents of this view believe that verse 11 presents an additional qualification for male deacons, one that must be considered at the time of their examination for church office:

> And let them [male deacons] also be tested first; then let them serve as deacons if they prove themselves blameless. [*Gynaikas*] likewise must be dignified, not slanderers, but sober-minded, faithful in all things. (1 Tim. 3:10–11)

155

DEACONS AS OFFICIAL ASSISTANTS TO THE ELDERS

In Chapter 3, *diakonos* was shown to be used in 1 Timothy 3:8–12 in the sense of assistant. The use of *diakonos* in this sense indicates one who carries out the will of another, such as a subordinate carrying out the assignment of a superior. The use also indicates that *the subordinate has full authority to execute the superior's delegated task*. So, as church officeholders and assistants to the elders, deacons exercise authority and supervision within the congregation as delegated representatives of the elders.

If the identity and role of the deacons have been correctly explained in Chapters 3 and 4, then the women referred to in verse 11 are most likely the wives of the assistants to the elders, and not assistants to the elders themselves.

If these women are deacons, they most likely share the same office with their male counterparts, *assistants* to the elders. Women as full-fledged deacons is one of the most popular and defensible of the other four views of verse 11. The all-Christian-women view is almost universally rejected by scholars, and the women-helpers-of-the-deacons interpretation has gained few supporters, but is not an impossible interpretation. This leaves deaconesses (a separate, third office) as a popular choice, but a much less defensible view than women as full-fledged deacons.

1 Timothy 2:9–15

If the women of verse 11 are deacons equal to their male counterparts, they are then made to be the overseers' *assistants*. But the idea of women assistants to the elders conflicts with the entire preceding context of 1 Timothy 2:8–3:7, particularly verse 12:[1]

> I desire . . . likewise also that women [*gynaikas*] should adorn themselves in respectable apparel, . . . [and] with what is proper

for women who profess godliness—with good works. . . . I do not permit a woman [*gynē*] to teach or to exercise authority over a man; rather, she is to remain quiet. For Adam was formed first, then Eve; and Adam was not deceived, but the woman [*gynē*] was deceived and became a transgressor. (1 Tim. 2:8–10, 12–14)

1 Timothy 2:8–15 is part of the overall context beginning in 2:1 and ending in 3:16. Paul's instructions on Christian men and women in the gathered assembly (vv. 8–12) are intimately connected to, and govern, his instructions for the overseers and deacons of 3:1–13.

Furthermore, Paul's directive against women exercising authority over men in the local church (1 Tim. 2:12) conforms to his overall teachings on the distinct roles of Christian men and women in the home and in the local church (1 Cor. 11:2–16; 14:33–38; Eph. 5:22–33; Col. 3:18–19; Titus 2:4).

In light of Paul's explicit restrictions in 1 Timothy 2:9–15, it is doubtful that the women of 1 Timothy 3:11 are women deacons in the sense of being equal partners with the male assistants to the elders.

Most commentators and church leaders who are committed to women deacons and/or deaconesses hold that the deacons are simply servants of the church, authorized by the church to serve the congregation in special ways. They may call the deacons "exemplary servants" or "leading servants." They would contend that 1 Timothy 2:12 does not apply to women deacons/deaconesses because they do not conduct the teaching of the church and are not official assistants to the elders exercising authority over men.

But this study has argued that the deacons are the official assistants to the elders, working in close association with the elders, and authorized by them to be their agents within the church. *How people view the office of deacon will be a significant factor in interpreting who the* gynaikes *are.*

No Distinctive Title

Another reason—and it is a significant one—for viewing the women of verse 11 as the wives of the deacons is Paul's very choice of the word *gynaikas* (women/wives) rather than a specific title, e.g., *women deacons* (*gynaikes diakonoi*). If these women are deacons (= assistants), calling them *gynaikes is an odd, ambiguous, and even inconsistent way to refer to church officials.*

Previously, Paul gave specific names to the two officers, *overseer* (*episkopos*) and *assistants* (*diakonoi*). But for the women in verse 11, he chose the general designation *gynaikas* (*women/wives*) without any modifying word or phrase to explain clearly their relationship to the male deacons. Patrick Fairbairn, a Scottish theologian and commentator who defends the view of women deacons, honestly admits that this is difficult to explain:

> It still is somewhat strange, however, that the general term *women* (*gynaikas*) is employed, and not the specific *deaconesses* (*tas diakonous*), which would have excluded all uncertainty as to the meaning.[2]

Phoebe a *Diakonos*

In Romans 16:1 Paul referred to a woman named Phoebe as *diakonos*. The *New International Version* renders *diakonos* as "deacon": "I commend to you our sister Phoebe, a deacon of the church in Cenchreae."

If, for the sake of argument, we suppose that Phoebe was a woman deacon, then Paul was not reluctant to use the term *diakonos* for a woman deacon. So, if Paul was singling out women deacons in 1 Timothy 3:11, why would he use the ambiguous and general word *gynaikas* and not *diakonous* with the feminine article—*tas diakonous* ("female deacons"), or *gynaikas diakonous* ("women deacons")?

Diakonoi for Both Men and Women

In the Greek language of the New Testament, there was no distinct feminine form of *diakonos*, such as *diakonē*. The Greek noun *diakonos*, although appearing masculine in its inflection pattern, is among a number of second declension nouns that can be either masculine or feminine.

Also, there was no special Greek noun for female deacons such as *diakonissa* (*deaconess*). The first recorded instance of the Greek word *diakonissa* (*deaconess*) appears some 260 years after the letter of 1 Timothy was written.

Since the inflectional pattern of *diakonoi* can be either masculine or feminine in gender, it can refer to women as well as to men. Although the *diakonoi* of verses 8–9 could include men and women deacons, the insertion of *gynaikas* in verse 11 strongly implies that Paul is referring only to male deacons in verses 8–9.

If the women are deacons like the male deacons, it would have been unnecessary for Paul to insert verse 11, which (again, according to the proponents of women deacons) states qualifications similar to those of verses 8 and 9. But there is nothing particularly gender specific about the qualifications listed in verse 11. If Paul was singling out women deacons for special mention, we would expect him to add some uniquely important qualifications for women deacons such as "the wife of one husband." But that is not the case.

Paul's Choice of the Words *Diakonoi* and *Gynaikes*

Paul was not, as some think, struggling for words or titles when referring to these women. He utilized the words *diakonoi* and *gynaikes* deliberately and precisely. He used *diakonoi* for male deacons in verses 8–10, and then in verse 12, he again used *diakonoi* for male deacons. Between these two clear designations (*diakonoi*), Paul intentionally employed the word *gynaikas* to identify these persons as "wives" of the *diakonoi*. "Wives" is an acceptable translation of *gynaikas*. It states immediately for the reader that the persons of verse 11 are wives of the deacons. Most English Bibles translate the Greek word *gynaikas* as "wives."[3]

THE PLACEMENT OF *GYNAIKES*

Another reason for thinking that the *gynaikes* are "wives" is the placement of the term in the middle of Paul's instructions on male deacons, rather than the placement of "[*gynaikas*] likewise" by itself, for instance, after verse 12:

Male overseers
3:1–2: If anyone aspires to the office of overseer, he desires a noble task. Therefore an overseer must be above reproach, the husband of one wife.

Male assistants (assuming women are not included)
3:8, 10: Deacons [males] likewise must be dignified. . . . And let them [male deacons] also be tested first; then let them serve as deacons if they prove themselves blameless.

Gynaikas
3:11: [*Gynaikas*] likewise must be dignified, not slanderers, but sober-minded, faithful in all things.

Return to Male assistants
3:12: Let deacons [males] each be the husband of one wife, managing their children and their own households well.

It would seem strange if Paul addressed male deacons in verses 8–10, then interjected four qualifications for what are assumed to be women deacons/deaconesses in verse 11, and then reverted immediately (as an afterthought?) to the marital and family qualifications of the male deacons. But to be fair, such an afterthought is not without precedent in Paul's writings (see 1 Cor. 1:14–16). If verse 11 refers to the deacons' wives and not to women deacons, verse 12 is not treated as an afterthought or a return to male deacons after speaking of women deacons in verse 11.

According to verse 10, deacon candidates must be publicly examined by the church and its leaders and proven "blameless" before they serve as the elders' assistants. The rendering "wives likewise" does flow nicely out of verse 10, indicating that the wives must be "dignified," like their deacon husbands. Based on this rendering, the deacon candidate's wife, then, would be included in the examination of the candidate's public reputation.

The Omission of Any Marital or Family Requirements

Another reason for favoring wives over women deacons is this: A faithful marital reputation was a matter of considerable importance to Paul. In the qualifications for elders and male deacons, Paul was emphatic: They were to be men with a reputation of being a one-woman kind of man. These men must each be "the husband of one wife." Moreover, Paul required that even a church-supported widow be "the wife of one husband" (1 Tim. 5:9).

But in verse 11, no direct instruction on the marital reputation of the *gynaikes*, such as "the wife of one husband" was set. No parallel marital qualification was made to match the male deacon's qualification (v. 12). Furthermore, no requirements are listed about their children or family life as required of the elders, male deacons, and dependent widows. It is difficult to conceive that Paul would require elders, male deacons, and dependent widows to meet the qualification of marital faithfulness, but not women deacons.

It is pure guesswork to assume that the omission of these requirements indicates that these women deacons/deaconesses/helpers were unmarried women serving the special needs of the women of the church. So much of what is said about the work of these women in verse 11 is nothing but speculation. What is clear is that nothing is stated in the text about their functions, only their character qualities.

The Deacons' Qualifications (vv. 8–9) and the Women's Qualifications (v. 11)

It is claimed by some that the women's qualifications in verse 11 parallel the male deacons' qualifications in verses 8–9. Indeed, some claim that verse 11 is an "abbreviated mirror of 3:8–9."[4] This suggests to some that the women of verse 11 are the same as the deacons of verses 8–9.

The four qualifications listed for the women in verse 11, however, are both similar and dissimilar to the male deacons' qualifications in verses 8–9. There is no parallel qualification in verse 11 with "not greedy for dishonest gain" in verse 8. The so-called parallelism between verses 8–9 and verse 11 does not prove that the women of verse 11 are deacons/deaconesses. In fact, the similarities and dissimilarities of qualifications between verses 11 and verses 8–9 fit just as well with the wives-of-the-deacons view.

PHOEBE A *DIAKONOS* OF THE CHURCH

Many students of Scripture believe Phoebe to be an example of a woman deacon:

I commend to you our sister Phoebe, a servant [*diakonos*] of the church at Cenchreae, that you may welcome her in the Lord in a way worthy of the saints, and help her in whatever she may need from you, for she has been a patron of many, and of myself as well. (Rom. 16:1–2)

The problem is that it is not clear what is meant by the phrase "a [*diakonos*] of the church." There are five suggested interpretations. Phoebe was

- a full-fledged deacon of the church,
- a deaconess of the church,
- the pastor of the church,
- a servant of the church,
- a courier of the church in Cenchreae.

See www.deaconbook.com where I address each of these views in detail and argue for Phoebe being either an outstanding servant of the church or an official representative or courier of the church in Cenchreae traveling to Rome.

If there were women deacons/deaconesses in the first churches of Ephesus and Cenchreae, it is truly remarkable that we do not see a clear record of these women deacons/deaconesses and their prescribed duties in post-apostolic Christian literature for more than 150 years after the time of Paul. And when such records do appear, they are mostly in the eastern churches.[5] Moreover, in Rome there is no evidence of women deacons for hundreds of years after Paul's letter to the Romans.[6]

OBJECTIONS TO THE WIVES-OF-THE-DEACONS VIEW

Regardless of how one interprets verse 11, problems and perplexing questions plague each interpretation. We thus need to address three objections that are commonly raised against the wives-of-the-deacons view.

1. The Omission of the Pronoun or Article with *Gynaikas*

If Paul was referring to deacons' wives, why did he omit the possessive pronoun *their* (*autōn*), or the definite article (*tas*), or both the definite article and pronoun? If he had written "their *gynaikas*" (*tas gynaikas autōn*), we would know with certainty that the women were the deacons' wives.[7] This is a fair criticism and the strongest objection to this view.[8]

As previously stated, Paul addresses male deacons in verses 8–10, and "[*gynaikas*] likewise" follows immediately. Then Paul returns to addressing male deacons, whom he requires to be "the husband of one wife." The *gynaikes* (women/wives) cited in the middle of this section on male deacons (most of whom were husbands) does suggest that *Paul is referring to women in closest relationship to the male deacons*, that is, "wives." The full context of verses 8–10 and 12 on male deacons only helps clarify the identity of the *gynaikes*. Verse 11 becomes another qualification required of the male deacons: "wives likewise must be dignified." Thus, although the possessive pronoun or article would be most helpful, it is not absolutely necessary in this context on male deacons.

A similar problem occurs with the use of the title *diakonoi* in verse 8. No definite article or possessive pronoun is attached to *diakonous*. It is anarthrous (without the article). If Paul had added the possessive pronoun "their" to *diakonoi*, we would know with certainty that the *diakonoi* were the overseers' assistants. But Paul did not add a definite article, possessive pronoun, or modifying phrase, such as, "of the poor" or "of the church." It is the *diakonoi*'s association with the overseers, their character qualities similar to those of the overseers, and the possible meaning of *diakonoi* as assistants that identify the *diakonoi* as the overseers' assistants.

In the end, it is easier to explain the omission of the pronoun "their" than it is to explain why Paul used the general term *gynaikas* ("women/wives" in v. 11) instead of a specific term, *tas diakonous*, or *gynaikas diakonous* (women deacons).

2. Content and Grammatical Structure of the Passage

Some also contend that the content and grammatical structure of the passage require that the women of verse 11 be officeholders like the deacons. Verse 11 is introduced by the adverb "likewise," which parallels the adverb "likewise" in verse 8, "deacons likewise must be." The words "must be" in verses 8 and 11 are appropriately supplied by the Bible translators from verse 2, connecting this entire passage grammatically and conceptually:

> **Verse 2:** Therefore an overseer must be (*dei . . . einai*) above reproach.

> **Verse 8:** Deacons likewise [must be] dignified; ("must be" is supplied from verse 2).

> **Verse 11:** Women likewise [must be] dignified; ("must be" is supplied from verse 2).

Accordingly, the introductory adverb "likewise," and the dependence of verses 8 and 11 on the words "must be" from verse 2, signal that three distinct groups are addressed. Many Bible students understand this to mean that Paul was referring to women officeholders in verse 11. So, when the designation *gynaikas* appears in verse 11, although there is no modifying word, phrase, or article attached, they argue that the context and the grammatical structure of the passage require the interpretation that these women be officeholders like the deacons.

Clarifying the Use of "Likewise": The introductory adverb "likewise" means "similarly," or "in the same way." It introduces a new, distinct group of people (*gynaikas*, women/ wives) who are compared with the previous group, that is, the male *diakonous*. The grammatical construction of the passage linked by the adverbs "likewise" in verses 8 and 11 does not necessarily rule out the interpretation of "wives." The women of verse 11 are distinct from the male deacons (vv. 8-9), yet they are closely related and must be, like the male deacons, "worthy of respect" (NIV).

The phrase "[*gynaikas*] likewise must be" does not require that the women of verse 11 be *equally* church officeholders with the deacons of verses 8–10. There are other legitimate options. It has been proposed, for example, that the women of verse 11 are women helpers who assist the deacons in some way without having an official title, and that would explain why they are not called "deacons"—they had no official title. Or, they could be the wives of the deacons who officially assist their deacon husbands in their work.[9] The grammatical construction of the passage (vv. 2–12), especially the second use of "likewise," can be used to defend any of the views just presented. The translation "wives likewise must be" does not violate grammar or context. It is a legitimate interpretation and would form an integral part of the male deacons' reputations, qualifications, and examinations.

3. The Omission of the Elders' Wives' Qualifications

If the deacons' wives must be of a certain godly character, should not such requirements be even more necessary for the elders' wives? Some argue that the absence of a list of specific qualifications for the elders' wives (in vv. 2–7) is another key indicator that verse 11 refers to women deacons, deaconesses, or helpers.

Some interpreters argue that while there is no need for the

elders' wives to be mentioned, the deacons' wives are mentioned because part of the deacons' duties involve the care of widows and the poor, requiring the deacons' wives to be more directly involved in helping their husbands in their work. In his commentary on the Pastoral Epistles, George Knight contends that the best reading of the structural and difficult syntactical evidence of the passage is that the women referred to in verse 11 are the deacons' wives who officially assist their deacon husbands with the care of the church's widows and other needy women.[10] In the case of the elders' wives, assisting their husbands in their primary duties of teaching the Word would be prohibited (1 Tim. 2:12). Therefore, Paul did not list the qualifications for the elders' wives.

Others have proposed that the wives in verse 11 include the elders' wives. If a deacon's wife must be worthy of respect, it should be assumed, even though not stated directly, that an elder's wife must also be worthy of respect. If the wives of the deacons, the lesser office, must be of a certain moral character, the same principle should apply to the wives of the elders, the higher office. Certainly, an elder's wife must be worthy of respect and of good character. For instance, she cannot be a malicious slanderer, or she will damage her husband's reputation and the credibility of the entire eldership.

Verse 10 does seem to allude to the overseers of verses 2–7. Verse 10 implies that just as the overseers are to be examined for office (see 1 Tim. 5:24–25), so too, the deacons ("also") are to be examined as to their qualifications for office (see Chapter 6 for details). All the qualifications for the deacons apply to the elders as well, and most are similar to the elders' qualifications.

Furthermore, the elders must manage their households well (vv. 4–5). If an elder's wife is creating scandal, her behavior is offensive, or her character is seriously flawed, that elder's household is not "above reproach." Although the elder's wife is not mentioned in verses 2–7, *any serious assessment of a prospective elder's qualifications for office will include an evaluation of his wife and children to whom his public reputation is intimately tied.* It should be assumed that whatever is required of a deacon's wife needs also to be required of an elder's wife.

Another factor to consider is that the false teachers had made successful inroads into some of the female population of the church (1 Tim. 5:6, 11–15; 2 Tim. 3:5–7). This alarming situation may have compelled Paul to address the deacons' wives. Their godly character and reputation were essential to the public reputation and work of the deacons, so they had to be level-headed, respectable, trustworthy in every way. These qualities would certainly be expected of the elders' wives, but possibly had become a neglected aspect of the deacons' fitness for office. Paul did not intend to let this be forgotten.

The expectation that an elder's wife be of good character may be implied in the general qualification "above reproach" and in the logic of verse 5: "If [an overseer] does not know how to manage his own household, how will he care for God's church?" But in the case of a deacon, such a requirement may not have been assumed. Paul wanted to make perfectly clear that, as assistants to the elders, the deacons must have wives of good character.

Thus, when deacons are examined for office (1 Tim. 3:10), the reputation of their wives must also be considered in the examination process. The fact that a deacons' wife must be worthy of respect reinforces the importance of the deacons' position and work. I would conclude that *the public reputation of both the elders' and deacons' wives must be considered in the examination process. In fact, this is what, in practice, is done by all responsible churches.*

Whatever the reason for the absence of specific requirements for the elders' wives (and we may never know why), the omission does not present a decisive argument against the position that the deacons' wives are the women referred to in verse 11.

CONCLUSION

As with any difficult passage of Scripture, the arguments for differing interpretations go back and forth endlessly. There is no one grammatical point that is decisive in determining the identity of these women. Indeed, some interpreters think that the lack of information and the ambiguity of the language prevent us, or should prevent us, from determining their identity. Certainly, the difficulties prevent us from being dogmatic.

On the other hand, in trying to fit all the aspects of this textual puzzle together, I conclude that the translation "wives" allows most of the pieces to fit together best, as it is the simplest and most natural interpretation, and demands the least amount of guesswork. The deacons are assistants to the elders, and the women of verse 11 are their wives, who also must be "dignified."

As stated in Chapter 7, whether this passage addresses the deacons' wives, women deacons, deaconesses, or helpers, Scripture directs all Christian women to be actively engaged in "the work of ministry, for building up the body of Christ" (Eph. 4:12).

---

[1] For a must-read exposition of 1 Timothy 2:11–15, see Andreas J. Köstenberger and Thomas R. Schreiner, *Women in the Church: An Interpretation and Application of 1 Timothy 2:9–15*, 3rd ed. (Wheaton, IL: Crossway, 2016).

[2] Patrick Fairbairn, *Pastoral Epistles* (1874; repr. Minneapolis, MN: Klock and Klock, 1976), 150.

[3] "Wives": KJV, NKJV, NIV (1984), ESV, CSB, Goodspeed, Phillips, Moffatt, Godbey, NET Bible, GNT, NLT, NEB.

[4] Jennifer H. Stiefel, "Women Deacons in 1 Timothy: A Linguistic and Literary Look at 'Women likewise' (1 Tim. 3:11)," *NTS* 41 (1995), 450. See also, Jamin Hübner, *A Case for Female Deacons* (Eugene, OR: Wipf & Stock, 2015), 32.

[5] There is a second-century letter, written in Latin, from Pliny, the governor of Bithynia, to the Roman Emperor Trajan (ca. AD 112), that some scholars claim demonstrates that women deacons existed early in the second century. However, as in Romans 16:1, it is uncertain who these women were or what they meant to say under forceful

interrogation by Pliny, or what Pliny himself understood the slave women [Latin, *ancillae*] to mean by the term *ministrae*. For more information go to www.deaconbook. com.

[6]In the highly influential church order manual, *Apostolic Tradition* (ca. AD 215–20), which was written from Rome by Hippolytus, all the various offices of the church in Rome were listed. Hippolytus spoke of overseers, elders, deacons, subdeacons, confessors, widows, lectors, virgins, healers, but not of female deacons (Geoffrey J. Cuming, *Hippolytus: A Text for Students* [Brancote Notts: Grove Books, 1976], 8–15). Aimé Georges Martimort comments:

> The ecclesiology of St. Hippolytus of Rome simply excluded the possibility of deaconesses, as did the ecclesiology proclaimed by Tertullian all his life as well (*Deaconesses: A Historical Study*, trans. K. D. Whitehead [San Francisco: Ignatius Press, 1982], 32).

[7]The ESV and other translations add the word "their" to *gynaikas*, but "their" is not part of the original Greek text.

[8]See especially Barry L. Blackburn, "The Identity of the 'Women' in 1 Tim. 3:11," *Essays on Women in Earliest Christianity*, ed. Carroll D. Osburn, vol. 1 (Joplin, MO: College Press, 1993), 308–09. Blackburn sees the absence of the definite article or possessive pronoun as a key factor against *gynaikas* being wives. He lists only four occurrences of *gynē* or *gynaikes* without the article, but, in each case, *gynē* is in the singular, and the context makes clear that *gynē* is a wife (Mark 10:2; 12:19; Luke 18:29; 20:28; 1 Cor. 7:11).

[9]So George W. Knight III, *The Pastoral Epistles: A Commentary on the Greek Text*, NIGTC (Grand Rapids: Eerdmans, 1992), 170–72.

[10]Knight, *Pastoral Epistles*, 172.

Author Index

Scripture Index

179

General Index

Acknowledgments

Christian friends are a special gift from the good hand of God. I am an exceedingly blessed man to have many skilled friends who assisted me in the completion of this book.

All my books are a collaborative effort. There is nothing I do that I do not consult with many of my brothers and sisters and draw from the rich resources found in Bible commentaries. As the Scripture says, we need "strength to comprehend *with all the saints* what is the breadth and the length and height and depth, and to know the love of Christ that surpasses knowledge" (Eph. 3:18; italics added). It is with "all the saints" that I have written this book.

I gladly acknowledge special friends who have followed me from the beginning of this project. I am indebted to Rick Carmickle for his assistance and help throughout the long process of producing this book. Special thanks to Dick and Anne Swartley who donated endless hours to reading, correcting, and editing this book. A great deal of gratitude is extended to Jay Brady, Operations Manager at Lewis & Roth Publishers, who helped me at every phase of the production of this book. Without the help of my gifted Administrative Assistant, Lisa Corbett, I would still be in the process of writing this book. I am grateful for Lisa's work in checking sources, verifying quotes, documenting footnotes, and much more. Much thanks is also due to Amanda Sorensen and Allan Sholes for their final editorial work.

I have asked a number of scholars to evaluate the exegesis, arguments, and interpretations in this book. They have made significant contributions to the technical aspects of this work. Thanks to Michael Harris for checking my uses of the post-apostolic writers, Jack Fish for his expertise on all the Greek terms and grammar, Clarence D. "Jimmy" Agan III for his enlightening work on the *diakon-* word group, and Robert P. Gordon and Phil Faris for their many suggestions and warnings.

I gladly acknowledge and thank all those who helped by reading the manuscripts and providing me with comments. You know who you are.

As always, my deepest appreciation goes to my loving wife Marilyn, my chief partner in life and in the work of the Lord.

PAUL'S VISION FOR THE DEACONS

BIBLICAL
ELDERSHIP
RESOURCES

An Invaluable Online Training Program for
Equipping Elders Worldwide
www.biblicaleldership.com

"The lack of elder training is an extremely critical problem. We are
not training the very men who lead and have oversight of our churches.
We erroneously believe that our serving elders and deacons understand
spiritual oversight and care, but in fact our churches are filled with
elders and deacons who confess that they are unprepared and
untrained for their work."
— Alexander Strauch
in *Biblical Eldership Study Guide*

Working with a team of godly elders, Alexander Strauch has been instrumental
in launching a new online tool for training and equipping elders within
local churches worldwide. Utilizing the power of the internet, Biblical
Eldership Resources offers systematic elder training, in order to develop
present and future generations of local church elders across the world.
No other online training tool comes close the comprehensiveness of BER.
All the instructional material on the website is rooted in Bible exposition.

The materials and curriculum available on this website are designed
to be used by individuals or by small groups. So, visit the website and choose
the resources that best fit the needs in your church or your personal ministry.

Lewis & Roth Publishers
800.477.3239 ♦ www.lewisandroth.com

ADDITIONAL RESOURCES FOR PASTOR ELDERS

Biblical Eldership
by Alexander Strauch

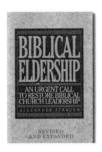

With more than 200,000 copies in print and translated into more than 20 languages, *Biblical Eldership* is a comprehensive look at the role and function of elders, bringing all the advantages of shared leadership into focus. *Biblical Eldership* explores the essential work of elders, their qualifications, their relationships with each other, and each of the biblical passages related to eldership. Written for those seeking a clear understanding of the mandate for biblical eldership, this book defines it accurately, practically and according the Scripture.

"Best exegetical overview of eldership around today."
— Kevin DeYoung, Pastor
Christ Covenant Church, Matthews, NC

"For churches to thrive they need to be led by men who follow the Scriptures. Strauch wonderfully instructs us on the character qualifications needed to serve as elders and the responsibilities incumbent on elders. This book is a valuable resource for courses on pastoral ministry and is highly recommended for every church."
— Thomas R. Schreiner, Associate Dean
The Southern Baptist Theological Seminary

"…[This] excellent book … is the definitive work on the subject….The book deserves wide distribution and I plan to do whatever I can to insure this."
— William MacDonald, Author
Believer's Bible Commentary

Additional resources for training and equipping elders:

- *Biblical Eldership Study Guide*
- *Biblical Eldership Mentor's Guide*
- *Biblical Eldership Booklet*
- *Biblical Eldership Discussion Guide*

Lewis & Roth Publishers
800.477.3239 ♦ www.lewisandroth.com

ADDITIONAL RESOURCES FOR
ONGOING DEACON DEVELOPMENT

Agape Leadership
by Alexander Strauch and Robert L. Peterson

Agape Leadership promises to be one of the most spiritually inspiring books you have ever read. R.C. Chapman (1803-1902) provides an extraordinary example of Christ-like, loving leadership. Charles Spurgeon, who knew Chapman, said of him, "the saintliest man I ever knew."

Chapman became legendary in his own time for his gracious ways, his patience, his ability to reconcile people in conflict, his kindness, his absolute fidelity to Scripture, and his loving pastoral care. By the end of his life, Chapman was known worldwide for his love, wisdom and compassion. In *Agape Leadership*, you will see godly, pastoral leadership in action through these biographical snapshots from Chapman's life.

"This book . . . should be read by everyone who calls on Christ as Lord. In so doing, you will be challenged to arrange your life in such a way that you are finding Christ to be your greatest and first love."
— Terry Delaney, Christian Book Notes

Meetings That Work
by Alexander Strauch

Are your elders' and deacons' meetings satisfying and productive, or do they drag on with little accomplished? Do you find it hard to stay on track when discussing important issues? Does your group spend too much time on trivial matters?

Meetings That Work will help bring vitality to your meetings and strength to your relationships as you work through the storms and struggles of normal church life. Short and practical, this book will lead to immediate improvements in your meetings.

"As usual Strauch writes as a man with a deep heartfelt desire to see elders take seriously their responsibilities and lead the church forward to the glory of God. Every elder should take the time to read this good book."
— Christian Education & Publications

Lewis & Roth Publishers
800.477.3239 ♦ www.lewisandroth.com

RECOMMENDED RESOURCES FOR
ONGOING DEACON DEVELOPMENT

If You Bite & Devour One Another
by Alexander Strauch

Conflict in churches is a pervasive problem we know all too well. In *If You Bite & Devour One Another*, Alexander Strauch examines the biblical passages on conflict and discusses key scriptural principles for handling various kinds of conflicts among Christians—whether personal disputes, issues of Christian liberty in lifestyles, congregational matters, or disagreements about important doctrines. The book emphasizes Spirit-controlled attitudes and behaviors through solid exposition and true-to-life stories of Christians handling conflicts in a Christ-honoring way.

"This book is urgently needed in the body of Christ. . . .I have put *Bite & Devour* into the top ten books that we are getting out across the world. It's a must read."
— George Verwer, Founder, Operation Mobilization

"This is a wonderful, profound resource for the Body of Christ. After much thought, I cannot think of a group of believers from the youngest all the way up to the elderly saints who would not benefit from this godly biblical counsel. It will be a much-used resource in my own life, home, and church."
— Gregory H. Harris, Professor of Biblical Exposition
The Master's Seminary

"This book is an excellent must-have resource for handling conflict. . . .What did I like about the book? Strauch has gone straight to where all Christians should go: the Bible. Just like the Bible does, Strauch calls us to change our attitudes and behaviors through the power of the Holy Spirit. . . . What do I not like about the book? That everyone has not read it."
— Noel Heikkinen, Pastor
Riverview Church, Holt, MI

Lewis & Roth Publishers
800.477.3239 ♦ www.lewisandroth.com

RECOMMENDED RESOURCES FOR ONGOING DEACON DEVELOPMENT

A Christian Leaders's Guide to Leading with Love
by Alexander Strauch

Alexander Strauch is a skilled Bible expositor. All of his books are based on the careful exposition of Scripture. In *Leading with Love*, Strauch presents all the New Testament passages on love and applies them to leading people according to the "more excellent way" (1 Cor. 12:31). Of special note is his powerful exposition of the fifteen descriptions of love from 1 Corinthians 13 and their application to Christlike leadership. You will be convicted, challenged and moved to lead by the "more excellent way," the way of Christlike love.

A study guide is also available, making this a valuable tool for group study.

"This message is urgently needed by all of us. You may have talents and spiritual gifts, but without the love that this book talks about, you don't really have much at all."
— George Verwer, Founder, Operation Mobilization

"*Leading with Love* is a superb exposition of how the followers of Incarnate Love should live out their love. I found it deeply challenging as, in simple, direct language, with apt quotes and illustrations, it probed one and another area of heart, soul and relationships with the insistent demand of the second of the greatest commandments."
— Robert Gordon, Faculty of Oriental Studies
University of Cambridge

"The Lord has truly blessed our ministry through this incredible and unique book on leadership."
— Tony Villanueva, State Director
Child Evangelism Fellowship of Oregon

Lewis & Roth Publishers
800.477.3239 ◆ www.lewisandroth.com